D1713495

MORE THAN MANY SPARROWS

Are not two sparrows sold

for a farthing? And yet

not one of them will fall

to the ground without

your Father's leave . . .

Therefore, do not be afraid;

you are of more value

than many sparrows.

St. Matthew 10:29-31

MORE

THAN

MANY

SPARROWS

LEO J. TRESE

FIDES PUBLISHERS, INC.

NOTRE DAME, INDIANA

CONTENTS

I. GOD'S LOVE FOR YOU   7

II. YOUR LOVE FOR GOD   14

III. THE VOICE WITHIN YOU   25

IV. THE STRENGTH WITHIN YOU   32

V. AS YOU ARE   39

VI. IF YOU ARE ANGRY   50

VII. THE POWER WITHIN YOU   61

VIII. THE WAY YOU GO   68

IX. THE WAY YOU WORK   79

X. THE WAY YOU LIVE   87

XI. THE WAY YOU LOVE   94

XII. THE GOOD YOU DO   105

XIII. RAISE UP YOUR HEART   113

XIV. GRACE IS WITH YOU   121

GOD'S LOVE FOR YOU

I

REGARDLESS OF WHAT our own personal problems may
be, there is one deep-seated need which all of us have
in common: the need to be loved and to *know* that we
are loved. We want to feel that what we do and what
happens to us, mean something to somebody else besides ourselves. Without this feeling that there is someone who cares about us and cares a lot, life at best will
be tasteless and at worst will be frightening—frightening even to the point of suicide.

Our Christian philosophy of life begins with the
conviction that, regardless of our human relationships,
there is Someone who does love us deeply and Who
does care intensely about what happens to us. That
Someone of course is God.

Early in our lives we learned that God created the
universe to show forth His infinite greatness and goodness. God's greatness is manifested in the almighty
power which fashioned the universe out of nothing,
by a mere act of the divine will. God's infinite goodness portrays itself in His decision to share His eternal

happiness with others, and His consequent creation of the human race.

That tells us why the world exists and why the human race exists; but it doesn't tell us why you and I exist as particular individuals. It doesn't tell us why God chose to make your soul and my soul in preference to any of the other possible souls, infinite in number, which God might have made instead. We have to remember that in the divine mind there are the images of an infinite number of souls which God could create if He so chose. Most of those images never will be called into existence. Why, we ask, did God choose to create you and me?

Turning to human imagery, we might compare God to a man who is looking through a book of house plans. Suddenly the man stops paging and puts his finger on the picture of a certain house. "There," the man says, "is just the house I want. That's the house I'm going to build." Similarly a woman might page through a catalogue of dress patterns. As her eyes fall on one particular model, they light up. "There," she says, "is a dress I really like. There is a dress I'm going to make."

Obviously God's decisions are made from all eternity. But speaking of God in human terms, we might say that God looked through the catalogue of "possible" souls in His divine mind. He passed by a billion billion others and stopped when He came to the image of you. "There," God said, "is a soul that I can really love. There is a soul that I want with Me forever in

8

heaven. There is a soul that I shall create." And so you came into being.

Because of God's infinite perfection our description is an inadequate one; actually God doesn't have to "stop and think things over." Yet the description is a true one. The underlying fact is absolutely true. God picked each of us out from an unlimited number of other possible souls because of a special and particular love for us. He wanted *you*, and nobody else would do.

God has never stopped loving you. Even in your moments of blackest ingratitude, your moments of darkest sin, God has not stopped loving you. As the mother of a wayward son never stops loving the child of her womb, neither does God ever cease to love the real you, the work of His hands, the particular image of Himself which you represent. God will hate your sin, but He will never hate you. Even when you may have turned away from God through sin, His love still presses upon you, trying to find a chink in your armor of self-love through which He may enter and turn you back to Himself.

It is a *personal* and an individual love that God has for us, too. We must not fall into the error of thinking that God loves us in an impersonal fashion, as just one little speck in the great mass of humanity. God does not lose sight of us, as you or I might lose sight of one drop of water in the vastness of the ocean. Because of His infinity, numbers mean nothing to God. If you were the world's sole survivor of an atomic war, God could not love you more personally than He does. At every moment you have His complete attention, His undivided love. At this very instant God is thinking of you, "looking at" you directly, loving you.

It is not enough simply to believe this with the mind. For any true and lasting happiness it must be the deepest conviction of your heart: that God does love you with a terrific love; that He is intensely aware of your present problems; that He cares tremendously about what happens to you; that out of your present burdens, imposed by the ignorance or malice of others (or by your own foolishness) God is going to bring good to you. It is the living certainty of this truth, of God's love for you, that must be the foundation of your Christian philosophy of life.

II

Where I read it, I do not now recall. I only remember that it struck me at the time as being the most pitifully stupid remark I ever had read. A man was undertaking to prove the depth of his love. "If you go to hell," the man said, "then I want to go to hell too." It was a remark that demonstrated the speaker's abysmal ignorance of the true nature of hell. Apparently he thought of hell as a place where two friends might sit hand in hand, comforting each other in their mutual misfortune. Hell is anything but that. Hell is a place of bitter loneliness, the lot of him who in life loved no one but

10

himself. There is no friendship in hell, there is no kin-
ship in hell. The only thing the souls in hell possess in
common is their hatred for each other and their hatred
for God, because hell is a state of unrelieved loveless-
ness—and the total absence of love is hate.

Just as this speaker (if he really made the statement)
had a totally mistaken idea of hell, so also do many of
us have a completely inadequate idea of heaven. Not
that any of us, in this life, can expect to have a truly
adequate understanding of heaven. But we have to
come as close to a real understanding as we can. Otherwise heaven is not worth living and working and suffering for. When the burdens of life press heavily upon
us, we shall be in peril of defeat and collapse. Of course
none of us is so childish as to think of heaven as a place
of pink clouds and twanging harps, or as a super coun-
try club where the sun always shines. We know that
heaven means eternal union with God. But if we do not
meditate on what that signifies, the knowledge will not
move us much.

We must try to imagine what it will be like to be
caught up in the embrace of Absolute Love, and to
find ourselves responding to the irresistible attraction
of that love with a force that will completely engage
our capacity for love. We think we know what it is to
love? We think we have experienced a great love—
for parent or child or spouse? Why, we haven't any
idea of what our real capacity for love is; we shan't
know it until the sight of God bursts upon us in the

11

moment of death or of release from purgatory. Trying to express it in human terms, we can only say that we shall find ourselves caught up in a wild, tearing torrent of love, a love of such violence that it seems to threaten our very existence. Indeed, if God did not give us the strength to absorb and to return His love, the piercing intensity of His infinite love would be more than any soul could stand.

As we see God as He is, in all His infinite lovableness, our own love will go out to Him in one great massive discharge. If there were time or room for amazement, we would be amazed at our undreamed-of capacity for love, the unsuspected depths of love within us which we never before had known or sounded. God's love will totally fill our soul like the vibrant sound of a great bell would fill a small room. Our love will answer to God in a breath-catching surge that is only short of pain.

It is this tremendous interchange of love that constitutes the essential happiness of heaven. We shall be united with God, merged with God, intermingled with God in an embrace of such perfect oneness as to leave strength or thought for nothing else. It will not be a tame or static sort of happiness. Looking (in vain) for human words with which to describe it, we can only say that it will be a dizzying, spiraling, heart-pounding, explosive sort of happiness. The prayer, "Eternal rest grant unto them, O Lord," is a plea for the departed souls which is hallowed by ancient usage, but we must be sure that this figure of speech does not mislead us in our concept of heaven. To one who is exhausted by struggles with temptation or by the hard knocks of the world, just plain restfulness may seem heaven enough. But heaven is not a place where we "just sit a spell." Heaven is not a state of quiescent idleness. In this life we never shall be as active as we shall be in that delirious moment of ecstasy when God becomes wholly ours, and we His.

"Moment," did we say? Yes, heaven is one supremely exquisite moment, but it is a moment that never ends. It is hard for us to grasp the fact that, beyond the physical universe, time ceases to exist. Time is the tool we use to measure the changes which the material world is constantly undergoing. When there no longer is any change, there no longer is any time. Eternity is not "a long, long time." Eternity is just one single instant, one grand and thundering NOW, a "now" that never ends. That is why we need not fear that we shall grow bored in heaven. Heaven lasts forever, but it is a forever that is compressed into one imperishable moment. Through millions of years the sun will cool and the planets will slow to stillness in their orbits. While all this is going on, there will be for you and me just this splendid and glorious instant, this pinnacle of consuming happiness, this our eternal moment with God.

II

YOUR LOVE FOR GOD

I

THERE CAN BE LITTLE HAPPINESS in our lives unless we have the conviction that life is purposeful. Everything which we do, consciously and willingly, we do with a purpose; there is a reason why we do it. Sometimes our purpose lies beneath the surface of consciousness, but it is present. This is true even of our apparently aimless actions. We stand idly looking out the window or pointlessly pacing about the yard. Actually we may be trying to settle our nerves, or trying to solve a problem in our minds, or perhaps unconsciously postponing a distasteful task that we should get at. It is characteristic of intelligent beings that their conscious behavior is *purposeful* behavior.

Since God is an intelligent Being—infinitely so—it follows that there is a purpose in all that God does. Since God is infinitely good, there must be a *good* purpose in all that God does. Consequently God must have created the universe and everything in it for a good purpose, with a good end in view. Everything that exists and everything that happens is going to

14

contribute to that purpose. Even events which to us seem insignificant, perhaps even unreasonable, nevertheless have a place in God's total plan.

Sometimes it is hard for us to accept this. It is such a small piece of life that we see. What will our own seventy or eighty years amount to, compared to the hundreds of thousands and perhaps millions of years during which God's plan will be working itself out? When an ant crawls across the rear wall of the Sistine Chapel at the Vatican, all that the ant can see is a bit of coarse paint beneath its feet. The ant (even if it had a human brain) could not realize that the bit of paint on which it stands is a part of that grand masterpiece of Michelangelo—the painting of the Last Judgment. Similarly, it is such a tiny bit of God's overall design that we see; it is no wonder that we sometimes are tempted to exclaim, "What reason could God possibly have for letting such a thing happen?"

Life is *purposeful*. We have to remember that. Day by day the world, and all who are in it, are moving forward towards the final fulfillment of God's plan. You and I are bristles on God's brush. Day by day we are adding our own little brush-strokes to the grand masterpiece, even though we shall not see clearly what our part has been until we see the finished product in heaven.

God wills that we, inspired by love for Him, should cooperate with Him freely and willingly. If we refuse to cooperate we shall hurt ourselves, but we shall not hurt God's plan. Even the evil that men do, God will use for His own purposes. God used the bitter hatred of the Pharisees for Christ, to effect the redemption of mankind. It well may be that God is using the evils of Communism to pave the way for the conquest of new nations and new peoples by Christ. Of this we can be sure: God's plan keeps moving forward. Every sparrow—yes and every wasp—has a place in it.

What this means for you and for me is that we should never surrender to the feeling that ours is an empty life, a purposeless life. God would not have made us if there had not been a special job that God wanted us to do. It is true that God made us because of the unique love He felt for us (humanly speaking) as He contemplated our image in His divine mind. But I think that surely one reason that God loves us so uniquely is because God saw that we could do a certain task for Him, and do it better than anyone else He might create.

From our own viewpoint it may be a very small thing, this special assignment that God has in mind for us; so often our viewpoint and God's do not coincide. The truth is that many of the big things we do, the big successes on which we are tempted to preen ourselves, are things that someone else might have done as well— or better. But there is something which we have to do for God which no one else could quite exactly duplicate. Perhaps it is some one person whom we have met or shall meet in the whole course of our life; some one person whom God had to reach (humanly speaking) through us or not at all. Indeed perhaps it is only one word which we have said or shall say; some one word which had to be spoken by us, or forever go unsaid.

That is why it is so important that we try to do well whatever we do, even our homeliest and dreariest tasks. That is why our personal relationships in particular must be motivated by great charity. We never know (in this life) the moment at which we are facing the task which is to be our special and exclusive contribution to God's plan. Everything which we do for God counts with Him, of course; everything is important. But there is some one thing that only we can do. It is this conviction of the special purposefulness of our own individual life that will save us from ever feeling that our life, even though lived on a level humble routine, has been a failure.

II

If we worry, we worry for one of two reasons: either we lack confidence in God, or we lack confidence in ourselves; perhaps even we lack confidence in both.

This is true no matter what the nature of our worry may be: fear of losing our job or of failing in our studies; anxiety about unpaid bills or about failing health; dread of not getting the girl we want or of losing the husband we have; apprehension about the behavior of our children or discouragement that we are not more popular or that we can't seem to "get ahead." These are but a few in the litany of human worries.

When we find that our facial muscles are settling into grooves and our digestive organs are getting tied up in knots, it is a sign that we have let our emotions take control of our intelligence. It is high time then to sit down to a spell of straight thinking, to the recollection of a few forgotten truths.

First of all God loves me. He cares intensely about what happens to me. He wants what is best for me. He is here with me right now, His whole attention fixed upon me. He is closer to me than any human being ever was or can be. And these are facts, real *hard facts*, not pious fables.

All right; so God cares about me. He is infinitely wise and knows what is best for me, down to the last tiny detail. He also is infinitely powerful. There is nothing that God cannot do. All creation is in the palm of His hand. This means then that God, Who wants what is best for me and knows what is best for me, doesn't have to stand helplessly by and watch me go down to defeat. God right this minute is at work at the very heart of my problem. God is manipulating these very circumstances which oppress and threaten me, so that in the end they will work to my advantage. I must believe this, or I do not know the true nature of God. I need to spend a long minute just looking at God, just making real to myself the fact that God, this God of love and wisdom and power, is not off in a distant heaven but that He is with me right here this very minute—and all the time. Then what am I worrying about?

Well, the catch is this: I do trust in God's care for me, but I also know that God expects me to do my part. He is not going to work miracles in order to accomplish what I ought to be doing myself. What really worries me is that I myself am failing. I just don't seem to have the knack of doing things right. It is my own mistakes—or fear of mistakes—that make me feel inadequate for this present task or responsibility. A smarter person would never get in the mess that I'm in; a more capable person would do so much better a job than I'm doing; a clever person would find a solution to this problem so easily. And *that* is why I worry.

Again it is emotion and not reason which is speaking. If I can honestly say that I am doing the best I can under these present circumstances, then God is one hundred per cent satisfied. He will take care of the rest, including the mistakes. In the end I shall be surprised to find how well everything worked out, although it did look so hopeless for a while.

I must remember too that the-best-I-can doesn't have to be a very good best. We human beings set very high standards for each other. If a boss assigns a job to one of his men, he expects the job to be done just as well as he might have done it himself. He makes his own

19

high standard the measuring stick for everyone else, and makes little allowance for lesser knowledge or ability. Parents sometimes show the same kind of over-expectation when dealing with their children. They give a child a task to do and then, forgetting their own greater maturity and experience, they criticize the child because the task is done imperfectly. This in spite of the fact that the child has done his best within the limits of his ability.

We can be grateful that God is not so demanding. Our best may be a very poor best, as full of mistakes as a sieve is full of holes; but if it is our best, even our reasonable best, then our performance is tops with God. He knows to the smallest fraction the extent of our native intelligence, the amount of our education, the handicaps (whatever they may have been) that entered into the formation of our personality. If He has steered us into a job, into a responsibility, into a tangle that seems beyond our ability, we can be very sure that He Himself is going to take care of the un-done parts. But we have to let God do it in His own time, in His own way.

To do the best we can and to leave the rest to God; this is the antidote to worry, the recipe for a tranquil heart.

III

It is not unusual to encounter persons who are troubled in mind because they do not seem to love God as they should. From one point of view, this is as it ought to be. We never can love God enough; we never can love Him as He deserves to be loved. We should be in a bad state if we began to feel that our love for God was sufficient, if ever we began to feel spiritually self-satisfied. There is a "divine discontent" that is essential to spiritual growth; a dissatisfaction with self that is a mark of spiritual health, much as the growing pains of childhood are the mark of normal physical development.

However, it is not the quantity but rather the quality of their love for God which occasions worry to some people. "Thou shalt love the Lord thy God with thy whole heart, and with thy whole soul, and with thy whole mind," Jesus tells us (Matt. 22:37). That seems a pretty definite command and it is addressed to all of us, not just to the saints.

Yet, if I really loved God with my whole heart and soul, shouldn't I *feel* it a little bit? Like I feel my love for other people—for my parents, my spouse, my children, my brothers and sisters, my friends? When love is strong, just hearing the name of the one we love can make our heart beat faster, can give a lift to the spirit. But I never catch my heart beating faster at the

21

mention of God's name, nor do I feel the least bit excited when I think of Him. Can I ever hope to make an act of perfect love for God? An act of perfect contrition? So runs the thinking of some troubled souls.

The weak spot in this chain of reasoning is that it confuses what we might call sentimental love with the pure love of spirit-for-spirit which is the basic nature of our love for God. The love of human-for-human almost always has an emotional content. It is a love which has a physical as well as a spiritual element. It is a love that we can *feel*, a love that we can to some degree measure by the intensity of our feeling.

It is not necessary however that there be any emotional content in our love for God. Real love for God resides in the *will*, not in the emotions. It resides essentially in the soul and only incidentally, if at all, in man's physical nature. It is true that some persons, especially many of the saints, have been able to feel their love for God in an emotional way. St. Philip Neri, for example, often would be seized with such violent palpitations at the thought of God, that his whole body would tremble from the wild beating of his heart.

This was a special and a precious grace which God gave to St. Philip, yet it was not this which measured the intensity of his love for God. Our love for God (as St. Philip's was) is gauged, not by how we *feel* towards God, but by what we stand ready to do for God. If in our mind and heart we are genuinely convinced that just *nothing* and *nobody* are to be preferred to God; if we honestly can say that, should duty to God demand it, we would be willing to separate ourselves from any human love, no matter how strong; if there is nothing that we have, position or possessions, that we ever would let stand between ourselves and God—then our love for Him is real.

Another criterion of our love for God is the extent to which the thought of God dominates our day. If we love God we live for God. This does not mean that we explicitly are thinking of God all the time—no more than a man consciously all day thinks of his wife and children, even though it is for them that (under God) he lives and works. If we are to have our mind on what we are doing, it is not practicable to be thinking of God consciously all the time. What it does mean is that always, just below the surface of consciousness, is the conviction that what we are doing, we are doing for God: our labor, our recreation, our family relationships, our social responsibilities— our whole sum of life. Once in a while during the day our thoughts may turn explicitly to God to make quick renewal of the morning's offering of our day to Him. Yet, even when He is not consciously in our thoughts, God will be in our heart and hands as we pursue the task of living.

It is quite possible to have a high degree of love for God and still to feel quite cold towards God as far as our emotions are concerned. The converse also is true. A person might feel pious even unto tears as the organ

23

plays softly in church, and yet go out and commit a mortal sin before the day is over. Our emotions just cannot be trusted as indicators of love. But, if we value God above all created things and persons; if we sincerely try day-by-day to live as He would have us live; then can we be sure that our love for God is authentic, regardless of how we may feel.

III

THE VOICE WITHIN YOU

I

FOR SOME PEOPLE the greatest obstacle to happy Christian living is a problem that lies within themselves rather than outside. It is the problem of a malformed or a poorly functioning conscience.

Conscience is an act of reasoning. It is a judgment made, here and now under these circumstances, as to what must be done as good or avoided as evil. If we act against our conscience and thereby sin, conscience continues its work; it condemns the wrong-doing and impels us towards repentance and amendment in order that we may reestablish peace within ourselves.

For a healthy conscience three ingredients are needed. The first of these is adequate knowledge of what *is* right and what *is* wrong. A person with little or no instruction as to the nature of his duties to God, to neighbor and to self, would be poorly equipped to make a right judgment as to the morality of any particular action. He might judge an action which is evil to be good, and an action which is good to be evil. His

25

unaided human reason might intimate that certain conduct was by its very nature right or wrong, but he
would be exposed to repeated errors in his judgments.

Besides knowledge, something else is needed for the
making of a healthy conscience. There are many people in and out of prison who know quite well what is
right and what is wrong, without letting the knowledge influence their conduct notably. They make their
decisions on the basis of what they themselves want
rather than on the basis of what God wants—and of
course miss happiness by a wide margin, frequently
with injury to others also.

Consequently, in addition to knowledge we need
to have a personal code of conduct which we have so
absorbed and made a part of us that it hurts us to go
against it. The merely speculative knowledge of what
is right and wrong must have been accepted by us and
woven into our total personality ("internalized" as the
psychologists say) so as to constitute a pattern of conduct against which we constantly measure ourselves.
This body of internalized ideals—"Myself as I ought
to be"—is the model upon which we keep our eyes as
we make our moral decisions and fashion our conduct.

Those who play an intimate part in the character
training of a child, the parents above all, are most
responsible for this aspect of conscience formation.
The child is quick to internalize the ideals presented
to him by the persons whom he loves and whom he
sees as loving him. It is from these same persons that

THE VOICE WITHIN YOU

a child learns the meaning of love. From them he learns
to love God, Whom he sees to some degree in their
image. In the beginning he internalizes ideals because
of his love for his parents; in time he is able to internalize ideals because of his love for God. A person
who sins and feels no guilt in his transgressions almost invariably will prove to be a person who in childhood was deprived of love. He may know intellectually what is right and what is wrong, but the ideal of
goodness never has become really a part of him.

Such persons sometimes can be made to conform
to a moral code by means of fear, and for the sake
of others control-by-fear is necessary when nothing
else will work. This is the philosophy behind our penal
system. However the decisive question with such persons never will be, "Can I do it and live at peace with
myself," but only, "Can I do it and get away with it?"

Along with knowledge and internalized ideals, there
is a third requirement for a healthy conscience: the
ability to think straight, the ability to reason with a
normal degree of clarity. This is where the God-given
virtue of prudence comes into play, that supernatural
help which enables us to form right judgments as to
what we should or should not do under this or that specific circumstance. We may know all the commandments and the complete list of our Christian duties; yet
no amount of religious instruction can give us cut-and-
dried answers to all the individual problems that will
face us. Life is too complicated for that. We have to

be able to take a moral principle and to apply it to a particular case.

It is a sin to lie and it also is a sin to hurt someone's reputation; if I am asked whether it is true that my next door neighbor is an alcoholic, what do I say? It is a sin to get angry and it also is a sin to neglect the training of my children; but they will not obey unless I get angry, so what do I do? It is a sin to associate with bad companions but if I am friendly to this person perhaps I can help him to become better; where does my duty lie?

Often in such apparent dilemmas I can seek and get competent advice. But when no other counsel is available and I must make the decision *now*, it is my reason illumined by grace and fortified by prudence that will point to the answer. Acting upon principles known and ideals embraced, my conscience will be my guide.

II

It is a sound conscience that enables us to steer a middle course between moral laxity on the one hand and scrupulousness or excessive rigorism on the other. A lax conscience will belittle the gravity of a moral offense, judging as non-sinful an action which in reality is sinful, or judging as venially sinful that which truly is a mortal sin. At the other extreme a scrupulous conscience may judge as sinful an action which in fact is innocent, or as mortally sinful a transgression which actually is venial.

Here we wish to discuss only the problem of scrupulosity. The well-intentioned reader to whom these words are addressed is not likely to suffer from a lax conscience. Moreover the remedy for a lax conscience is quite simple: consultation with a priest to correct false concepts of moral guilt, and humble submission to the teachings of the Church with respect to moral obligations.

A scrupulous conscience presents a much more intricate problem. Sometimes a scrupulous conscience may be the result of simple ignorance, as when a person mistakenly thinks it is a sin to say, "Oh hell," or to smoke a cigarette before Holy Communion. As soon as such a person's misconceptions are cleared up his scruples disappear. Such errors of conscience as these, stemming entirely from ignorance, really should not be termed scrupulousness at all. True scrupulousness is a much more serious malady.

Genuine scrupulousness is more of a psychological or emotional problem than it is a moral problem. A scrupulous person may know perfectly, in theory, the principles of morality and the relative gravity of various classes of sin; but he has lost the ability to judge rationally concerning his own conduct. Through physical illness, or through emotional or psychological disturbance, his reason has become clouded; at least as far as the morality of his own actions is concerned. If he swallows a bit of toothpaste he thinks he has broken his Eucharistic fast. If someone uses profanity

29

in his presence he thinks that he has sinned by listening. If he is tempted by unchaste thoughts he is sure that he must have sinned, even though he gave no consent to the thoughts. When he goes to confession he insists on telling the most minute details of real or fancied sins. After confession he is not satisfied that his confession was a good one; he is sure that he omitted some sin, or that he did not give sufficient details concerning some sin. He wants to go back to confession again and again, and even then finds no peace of mind.

The truly scrupulous soul is an unhappy person and one to be pitied. He needs the help of a physician or a psychiatrist much more than he needs the help of a priest. However his confessor can help considerably if he is willing to bind himself to give blind obedience to his confessor's directives.

For the majority of us, fairly well instructed in our Christian duties and with a normal capacity for passing judgment on our behavior, there are a few basic principles which will help us to resolve such occasional anxieties as may arise.

One such principle is that there can be no *unintentional* sin; we cannot sin without wanting to. Remembering this we shall not confuse temptation with sin. For example no matter how strongly we may be tempted with thoughts against chastity, we do not sin unless, recognizing the sinfulness of those thoughts, we willingly accept them into our mind and give consent to them.

30

Another principle that it is helpful to remember is that in case of an honest doubt (self-deception being excluded) I may give myself the benefit of the doubt, provided there is no way to dispel the doubt. Thus in case of honest doubt as to whether or not I have committed a mortal sin, I may receive Holy Communion without going to confession; taking the precaution of course to make an act of contrition for whatever guilt there may have been.

There are many applications of this principle of honest doubt. I may be doubtful concerning the law ("Is Holy Saturday an abstinence day?") or doubtful about the facts ("Is today an Ember Day?"). If there is no way to resolve the doubt then I may give myself the benefit of the doubt and act without sinning; in these instances I could eat meat. This supposes of course that harm will not result from a mistaken decision. Obviously a hunter may not shoot if he is doubtful whether it is a man or a deer behind the bush.

This principle of honest doubt does not mean that I may "take a chance" on committing sin. The state of mind of a person who says, "Maybe it's a sin but I'm going to do it anyway," is quite different from the attitude of the person who says, "I just don't know whether it is a sin and I can't find out; therefore it will be no sin for me to do it." In the first instance the person is quite willing to sin if it suits his purpose; in the second case the person acts only because his conscience tells him (rightly) that there will be no sin.

31

IV

THE STRENGTH WITHIN YOU

I

CONSIDERING HOW ESSENTIAL it is to a soundly happy life, it is rather surprising that we do not hear more about the virtue of prudence. Prudence is one of the four cardinal virtues, the other three being justice, temperance and fortitude. They are called the cardinal virtues from the Latin word "cardo" which means hinge. On these four virtues hinges our whole moral life, our peace of mind here and our happiness hereafter. Of the four, prudence is the most important because prudence enters into the practice of all other virtues.

For example, a person might sin against temperance by excess (gluttony) or by defect (harmful dieting); a person might fail in fortitude by excess (foolhardiness) or by defect (cowardice). In all the virtues it is the golden mean at which we aim, and it is the virtue of prudence which establishes the golden mean.

Prudence is defined as the virtue which disposes us to form right judgments as to what we must do or must not do under all circumstances. A prudent person is a person who is said to have good judgment. Prudence is both a natural virtue and a supernatural virtue. As a natural virtue prudence is acquired, like such natural virtues as honesty and truthfulness, in the process of character formation within our own home. There are persons who are "just naturally" prudent, as there are persons who are "just naturally" honest or truthful. That is the way they have been reared. They may have little or no religious belief, but they feel that certain kinds of conduct just aren't becoming to a decent human being.

As a supernatural virtue, prudence was infused into our soul along with the grace of Baptism. When we are in possession of supernatural prudence our natural judgment is assisted by divine grace. The basis of our judgments is different, also. We no longer make our choices or decisions merely in the light of what is most suitable to our nature as human beings; with supernatural prudence we form our judgments on the basis of what will be most pleasing to God Whom we love.

Supernatural prudence builds on natural prudence. Just as a baptized child has the virtue of faith but cannot exercise it until he learns the truths of faith, so might the supernatural virtue of prudence be hampered in its exercise by an inadequate foundation of knowledge and experience. Barring special grace, a poorly instructed Catholic cannot be expected to practice the supernatural virtue of prudence as effectively as one who knows his faith well. The maturity which is born of experience also will help.

Obviously there will be times when supernatural prudence does not agree with natural prudence. Natural prudence might say, "It's raining too hard to go to Mass"; supernatural prudence will say, "Get out the raincoat and umbrella; you can stand a little dampness for God." Natural prudence might say, "My child would have to cross a busy street to go to the Catholic school"; supernatural prudence will answer, "Moral danger is much worse than physical danger." Natural prudence might say, "We can't afford to have another baby now"; supernatural prudence will reply, "Only God has the right to decide whether or not a new life shall begin."

Our guiding light in the practice of prudence is the question: "What, under these circumstances, would God most probably want me to do?" If we can form the habit of acting always according to that principle, in little things as well as in big things, then we have taken a long step forward towards achieving peace of mind.

So much of our mental disquiet is occasioned by the fear that we may make the wrong decision in this matter or that matter. After the deed is done we worry as to whether or not we have acted wisely. However, when we go through the day looking at things from God's viewpoint, making His will (as well as we can see it) our will, we find ourselves making our choices and decisions with confidence and with mental ease.

And we never will be wrong. Even when, judging

by immediate results, we seem to have made a bad guess—it still is the right decision that we have made. As time passes we shall find that our apparent boner really was no boner at all; in the end it will prove to be the best thing we could have done. We can't ever be wrong, really, when we are right with God.

We must of course be scrupulously honest with ourselves in answering the question, "What would God probably want me to do?" Always there will be the temptation to blind ourselves to considerations that conflict with our own preferences, to try to twist God's will to conform with ours, to make God look at things through our eyes rather than make ourselves look through His. If we can clear this hurdle, then we have found the big answer to serenity of days.

II

No one can enjoy real peace of mind unless he has respect for himself; and no one can have respect for himself if he consciously compromises his conscience through fear of consequences. Anyone can be good when it is easy to be good. But God expects more of us than that. God expects us to be good even when it hurts—as so often it does. That is why we need the supernatural virtue of fortitude, one of the four cardinal virtues with which God has endowed all of us who are baptized.

Fortitude is the virtue which disposes us to do what

is good in spite of any difficulty. Just as supernatural prudence functions best when it is based on a foundation of natural prudence, likewise is supernatural fortitude practiced with greater facility when it is underlaid by a natural strength of character. The person who by nature is timid and fearful will find it harder to exhibit fortitude than the person who by nature is courageous. But this does not mean that the timorous person must of necessity surrender to his fears; to maintain that would be to deny the effectiveness of God's grace.

At its peak of performance fortitude is the virtue of martyrs, of those who have endured torture and death rather than to betray God by sin. It is unlikely that any of us will be called upon to practice fortitude to such a heroic degree. But, unless we are walled off from the world in some little hermitage of our own, it is likely that we are called upon to practice fortitude in small bits and pieces several times a week. Our world of work and of play is not particularly sympathetic to virtue. To be true to our conscience day-by-day, in small things as well as in big, often means a minor-key sort of martyrdom.

It is hard not to laugh at the obscene joke, especially if the teller happens to be the boss or a good customer. When the malicious gossip starts it is hard to insist on changing the conversation or to speak up in defense of the person under attack—especially when the person being discussed really is a stinker. It is hard to say "no" to the genial host who insists that we have just one more, although we know we have had more than enough to drink already. It is hard to make the boy friend keep his hands where they belong when "everybody says" that a little loving never hurt anyone—and especially when boy friends are so hard to get. It is hard to refuse to join the neighborhood group that is banding together to keep out the Negroes, especially when the moving spirits are such nice people and church-goers too. It is hard to drop out of the group that is going on from dinner to see the risqué play which has such wonderful acting. And it is so hard to be patient with stupid people and kind to unreasonable people and forgiving towards malicious and cruel people.

Yes, it *is* hard to be as good as we'd like to be when all the social customs seem to be pressuring us to compromise. But if we do not withstand the pressures, if we do not practice the virtue of fortitude, how else will the world be saved? In the pleasure-loving and success-hungry environment in which most of us live, the need is not for one or two heroic martyrs shedding their blood for Christ. The need is for a million or so pint-size martyrs who are willing to shed a few drops of nervous sweat for Christ in the offices and factories and neighborhoods, in the clubs and the PTA's; little martyrs who will be rallying points for the inherent decency which most people possess, but which so many people are afraid to show. So often a group will live in fear of each other's opinion; each one wishing that things could be different but each one afraid to make the first move.

If we shrink from the thought of becoming a reformer even in a small way, we should remember that most reformers who come a cropper do so because they do not temper their zeal with charity. No one likes to be preached at even when he knows he is wrong. Everyone resents a holier-than-thou attitude— having someone else's virtue thrown violently in his face.

Our own aim should be to do what is right ourselves, to do it courageously and consistently but quietly and without fuss. There is no need to look down our noses at others or to condemn others. A friendly smile and, "I'm sorry but I'm afraid I can't do that," is enough; if indeed any words at all are needed. Those who have been given to compromise often are surprised to discover, when they do begin to stand by their conscience, how they seem to grow in stature in the eyes of other people. They were so afraid that they would lose their friends; they find instead that they have gained respect as well as affection. They may not be as much fun at a party but they seldom are left out when plans are made; because their friends find in them such a source of strength for themselves. Fortitude has its rewards.

V

AS YOU ARE

I

IT IS A GREAT ADVANTAGE to be able to see yourself as you are, with clarity and with honesty; to see yourself as the product of God's creative handiwork, with limitations and talents equally a part of your endowment and your heritage. To be able to see yourself and to *accept* yourself as you are, without resentment or anxiety concerning your shortcomings and without complacency or vanity concerning your gifts: this is an essential ingredient to happiness—this is the virture of humility.

Humility is a magnificent virtue, but over the years the meaning of the word "humility" has undergone a sad deterioration. To many people humility means such things as timidity, fawning servility, abject submissiveness. In other words humility is equated with weakness, with an inability to stand straight and strong and to look up at the stars.

True humility is none of these things. Humility is synonymous with truth, with reality. The humble man (or woman) sees himself as he is: only a little less than

39

the angels, and yet with nothing at all that he can take
personal credit for. He is conscious of his obligation
to use well the talents that he has, since they represent
God's investment in him. He is not envious of others
who may possess talents which he himself lacks; let
them account to God for their own gifts—he knows
that he will have enough to do to account to God for
his. If he finds himself without any spectacular talents,
with just the universal human talents for goodness, for
love, for joy in his status as a son of God—he is content
in the knowledge that these are the big ones, the ones
that matter most.

There are two common misconceptions of humility
which might be noted here. One is the counterfeit humility of those who deny or belittle the talents which
they have. A simple example is that of the girl who is
asked to sing at the party. "Oh no," she says, "I really
can't sing; ask Joan, she sings ever so much better than
I do." This may sound like humility, but it more likely
is a perverted kind of pride. It is wrong to boast about
our talents as though we were personally responsible
for possessing them—but it is equally wrong to belittle
such talents as God has given us. We dishonor God if
we deny His gifts.

Another type of false humility is that of a person
who always is calling attention to his own faults or
defects. This sometimes is called "humility with a
hook." The trick is to depreciate oneself in the hope
of snaring a compliment. "I never seem to have much

luck with my cakes," says Mrs. Jones. "Oh Mrs. Jones, how can you say that? You bake such wonderful cakes." God knows our shortcomings and we (if we are humble) know them; that is enough. No purpose is served by beating our breast in public.

If we wish to make a rough check on the extent of our own self-knowledge, of our own humility, there are a few pertinent questions we might ask ourselves. "Am I charitable in speech?" is one such question. If I am critical of others, loving to point out their faults, it means that I am bragging about my own virtues by implication. Every time I critize another I am silently patting myself on the back and calling attention to the fact that I am not that way myself. Where there is lack of charity in speech, there is great lack of humility.

Am I patient with the mistakes and the failures of others? If I am quick to annoyance, quick to condemn others for their stupidity or their carelessness or their malice, it means that I have not looked very deeply into myself. It means that I have forgotten my own close calls, forgotten the many times I was saved from making a fool of myself only by the grace of God. It means that I take personal credit for being by nature more skillful, more conscientious or more virtuous than another. The humble man on the other hand never forgets that there is no height of folly and no depth of depravity of which he would not be capable if he had no resources but his own. The humble man never forgets that "there but for the grace of God go I"; as

41

a consequence he is a man of great patience and compassion.

Can I take criticism? It is not to be expected that I should *like* criticism; but when criticism does come, can I accept it gracefully and calmly without blowing my top, without being resentful or discouraged? If I really know myself, then I know whether or not the criticism is deserved. If the criticism is justified, then I accept it gratefully and profit by it, even though the critic may be an unfriendly one. If the criticism is undeserved, then I know my guiltlessness and so does God, the two who really matter. I may explain to my critic his error, but if I grow angry in doing so it means that I have the touchiness of the proud.

Charity, patience, serenity; if I have these then I am humble, and being humble, I am strong. It is the proud man who is vulnerable, it is the proud man who is weak.

II

It is easy to say, "Be prudent and you will be right." In fairness we have to admit that it is not easy to look at life with completely unclouded vision. The best of us have our prejudices, our character quirks, our defects of personality.

The degree of our mental health is measured by our ability to get along with people, to solve our problems, to accept frustration and even failure; in short, to adjust ourselves successfully to the ever-changing circumstances of life. The state of our mental health depends largely upon what happened to us in infancy and childhood. Our personality began to form the moment we were born. The pattern of its development was established by the nature of our relationships with the persons closest to us; above all by our relationships with mother and father.

If we grew up in a home where we had our own parents who loved each other and loved us, so that we *felt* loved and wanted and secure; a home where our parents steered a wise middle course between over-severity and over-leniency; a home where there was a minimum of discord and anxiety—then it may be taken as certain that we have a well-balanced personality. We get along well with people—with wife or husband, with boss and fellow-workers, with neighbors and with friends. We have a wholesome confidence in ourselves. We do not worry unduly, we accept defeat gracefully, we do not blow up at every little frustration. We can make a decision without too much agonizing, and we have a conscience that is neither lax nor over-rigorous. We still have our weaknesses, but we are reasonably happy most of the time.

On the other hand, we may have had a father who was tyrannical and unreasonable, or a mother who was domineering and over-possessive of her children. We may have had parents who favored one child over the other, or who compared one child unfavorably with

43

another. We may have been over-protected and "spoiled," or disciplined too severely. Our emotional development may have been obstructed by long childhood illnesses. Our home may have been broken by divorce or by some other factor.

The personality growth of a child is beset by many hazards. Fortunately God seems to have endowed us with a built-in stabilizer which enables us to survive, with little hurt, the minor hazards; the inevitable mistakes which even well-intentioned parents sometimes will make. If parents genuinely love each other and want and love their children, they can make a good many lesser mistakes without doing any real harm to their youngsters. A child can stand a lot of buffeting if he is sure that he is loved.

The point of all this is that many persons do suffer from personality defects which have their roots in infancy and childhood, defects which no amount of pure reasoning can eliminate. The roots are too deep and too obscure, experiences too painful to be maintained in conscious memory and long since repressed into the unconscious mind. A psychiatrist might help us to expose and to kill off these deep-imbedded roots. But psychiatric treatment is expensive; even if there were enough psychiatrists to go around, most of us would not have the money or the time to invest in such therapy—not unless our personality defect were so acute and so disabling as to leave us no other alternative.

So we have to learn to live with our personality

handicap, whatever it may be, as well as we can. A person who in childhood was stricken with polio and left with a permanently crippled leg or arm, does not therefore abandon all hope of a useful and a happy life. He learns to live with his handicap, to minimize its effects, to make still better use of the muscles and limbs that remain.

It may be that we did suffer some emotional hurt in childhood. We are self-conscious and find it hard to mix with people, or we are too hot-tempered and pugnacious, or we lack confidence in ourselves and are indecisive when decision is called for, or we are too impulsive and act without thought of consequences, or we are too jealous of our loved ones, or we have a punishing conscience which sees guilt where there is no guilt. We may have one of these defects, or one of a dozen others. That then is our handicap; what shall we do?

First let us admit that we have the handicap. It is as foolish to try to hide a personality defect from ourselves as it would be to try to hide a crippled arm. Then we shall ask God to help us to control the handicap so that it may not cause hurt to others, and we shall ask God for the grace to bear with what we cannot change—as His grace might help us to bear with arthritis or with migraine headache. We shall not accept defeat nor wallow in self-pity. Drawing upon our strengths we shall build around our weakness a satisfying and a constructive life. Above all we shall again

45

remember that in the end we are to be judged solely on the basis of how hard we have tried, as we are and with what we've got, to do the job at hand. To that standard anyone can measure up.

III

"Sometimes I get so discouraged." Do the words have a familiar ring? There are very few of us who have not spoken them at one time or another, at least silently to ourselves. They are the words spoken by a mother as she tries to keep up with the needs and the problems of her growing family. They are the words spoken jointly by husband and wife as they try to make the pay check stretch to meet the mounting bills. They are the words spoken by the heart-sick wife of an alcoholic husband. They are the words spoken by a teacher as she sits beaten at the end of the day, wondering why she ever set foot in a classroom. They are the words spoken by the person of good will who finds himself struggling with so little apparent effect against the same old temptations over and over again.

"Sometimes I get so discouraged." Surely the face of God must be touched with a compassionate smile as He hears these words from the lips of His children, rising day after day in every tongue and accent. He smiles because He knows that the ones who speak these words are most often the ones who mean them least. They feel discouraged, yes, for the moment. The stoutest limb will sometimes bend and creak beneath its burden of snow or ice or wind. But the limb springs back, and so too do these dejected hearts. Wearily perhaps, but doggedly, they take up their burden again and follow the rough path whose end, if it has one, they cannot see.

So God smiles—but with compassion. He is a Father with an unquenchable love for His children. He pities them in their distress. The sin which darkens the human mind and weakens the human will was not God's doing; it was man's own choice. The heavy load of suffering which so often is imposed upon the innocent by the ignorant, the weakness or the malice of others, is the inevitable consequence of sin. It is as inevitable as is the deadly fall-out which accompanies the hydrogen bomb.

God will not destroy the free will which He has given man. God will not step in to halt the chain reaction of sin and suffering which man has set in motion. What God will do and does do is to make certain that no burden which is borne for Him will crush the bearer, and that no pain which is sustained for Him will be wasted.

To feel discouraged occasionally, is quite human and quite to be expected in the lives of most of us. To feel discouraged is not the same thing as to *be* discouraged. To feel depressed is not the same thing as to be despondent. And of this we can be sure: at the moment when we feel at our lowest, at that very moment the God Who loves us is closest to us. We may not feel the lift that His hand gives to the cross on our shoulder, but how else is it that we are able to stand up once more and plod on?

That most often is God's way: not to take the cross away, but to help us carry it; and the heavier the load, the more of its weight will God bear. It seems strange, but did you ever notice that the people who would seem to have the most reason for despondency are usually the ones who are least discouraged? As a class, people who are incurably ill are among the most cheerful and courageous of persons.

So God gives the cross a little lift. And the mother gets up from her knees and says, "Well, let the new baby come. A new car would be nice but another saint some day in heaven will be nicer, even if I do have to wait a long time to see the day." And the father puts away his pencil as he says, "No beer money again this month, but we're not in the poorhouse yet; and thank God for that wonderful wife of mine." And another wife fingers her rosary as she looks at the drunken figure sprawled on the bed and says, "Well, if I was a nurse in an alcoholic ward I'd have a dozen like him to take care of and think nothing of it. He's my job, and the children and I will see him through this sickness if he'll let us." And the teacher dries her tears as she raises her head from the desk and remembers, "It's been happening like this for generations; some day they'll all be fine men and women even if they are such

48

stupid little beasts now; one of those little devils might even be a priest. I mustn't give up." And the soul struggling with temptation reminds himself again, "I *know* I can't lose if I just keep trying; God wants me to win even more than I want it. Back to confession again, and one of these days I'm really going to get over the hump."

The hardest part of our discouragement of course is our feeling of aloneness, our feeling that there is no one to lean on, that no one cares. If God would just give us a palpable pat on the shoulder and say in an audible voice, "You're doing a wonderful job, my child," it would be so much easier. But then we would not be the heroes (humble, pint-size heroes true enough) that heaven is filled with. God is not going to dilute the intensity of our final ecstasy for the sake of a moment's comfort now. But his hand is here, we must believe it; and His voice speaks to our heart.

VI

IF YOU ARE ANGRY

I

"I WONDER WHY GOD lets a man like that live?" The speaker was referring to a neighbor whose viciousness was bringing heartbreak to his family and fury to all with whom he came in contact. The answer to the question is of course that God lets this man live for the same reason that He lets any of us live: in order that he (and we) may have a chance for eternal life. As long as breath remains, there always is the hope that God's insistent grace may, even at the last moment, find entrance into the hard and perverse heart.

If God were to liquidate all criminals and sinners at the very onset of their first evil act, there would have been no St. Dismas, no St. Mary Magdalen, no St. Matthew, no St. Augustine. In fact our earth would be a lonely place indeed, and heaven quite depopulated. Would I myself be alive today? Maybe my sins and crimes are not the kind of stuff that newspaper stories are made of, yet there is no one but God who can draw a line and say where little evils leave off and big ones begin. It well may be that my many little unkindnesses

50

will be uglier, in the final judging, than some of the monstrous cruelties of the Stalins and the Hitlers. A martyr goes smilingly to his death for conscience's sake even as my neighbor cries herself to sleep because of a catty remark of mine.

As we question the justice of God in allowing cruelty and evil to abound, we need to remember that it is you and I who account for much of the world's unhappiness. Poverty is not the greatest evil. Poverty only hurts by comparison, only hurts when others around us are more prosperous; and even then poverty and happiness often go hand in hand. Neither is physical pain the greatest evil. A lot of happy spirits can be found in pain-racked bodies. The burdens that are hardest to bear are the burdens of wounded hearts, and it is to these burdens that so many of us make our own contributions.

I shall never forget the high school girl who, in my religion class, wondered aloud why God permits so much evil in the world. On the way in to class I had overheard that same girl say to another, in a fit of pique, "With that homely face of yours you'll never have a boy friend." All through the class period the second girl had her head down on what I am sure was a very damp desk. Yet the first girl saw no incongruity when she asked why God allowed evil in the world. It did not occur to her that if God did otherwise, she herself would be dead.

It is perhaps mankind's greatest tragedy that most

of the real unhappiness in the world is totally unnecessary. Adding up all the natural disasters, such as earth-
quakes, fires and tornadoes; adding also sickness and
poverty and even the occasional despot and warlord:
all of these put together would not equal in output of
unhappiness the misery that is caused by plain, ordinary human unkindness. We weep for the victims of
the Kremlin even as we pettily discharge our own
barbs on Maple Avenue and Lawncrest Drive.

"Bear one another's burdens, and so you will ful-
fill the law of Christ" (Gal. 6:2). This is the challenge
that St. Paul proposes to us: that we make ourselves
carriers of the tenderness and the compassion of our
Lord Jesus. It is for us to support rather than to weaken
the spirits of others, to mitigate rather than to aggra-
vate the unhappiness that we find around us.

So often in our own pain we lash out, like wounded
animals, with sarcasm and criticism and sharp rebuffs.
We inflict senseless injuries, perhaps, on those to whom
we most owe love, perhaps on those who already are
carrying more than their fair share of heart-heaviness
and inner pain. One would expect that, having suffered
ourselves, we would be doubly anxious not to inflict
unnecessary suffering upon others. Yet the sad fact is
that it seems to work just the other way. Whenever we
examine our conscience, a goodly part of our scrutiny
surely will be given to the question, "To whom, and
how often, have I caused unnecessary hurt?" And our
most earnest prayers surely will be offered for those

who have felt the sting of our heedless tongue and our sly cruelties.

Yes, God could have eliminated all suffering from the world simply by destroying Adam and Eve as soon as they had sinned. It would have been an empty world, but there would have been no unhappiness. Nevertheless God willed otherwise, knowing that man's present pain, sanctified by the agony of His Son upon the cross, would be a small price to pay for the ecstatic joy that is man's final destiny; knowing too the beautiful spectrum of charity that would arch the heavens as each of us, even in our own weakness, would reach out to lighten the burden of one another. It remains only for us to ask ourselves, "How much am I doing to add, even a little, to the happiness of others? Whose burden did I bear today?"

II

Certain types of illness may cause a person to be chronically irritable. Diabetes and high blood pressure sometimes have this effect. The mental illness called schizophrenia, particularly if it is of a paranoid kind, will result in an even higher degree of irascibility.

Aside from these exceptional instances there is the common garden variety of hot-tempered person, the person who is hot-tempered "by nature." Actually no one is hot-tempered by nature. A mean temper is not something we inherit. No one is born with it. The over-aggressiveness and the hostility which we commonly characterize as hot temper are acquired in the course of a person's infantile and childhood training. It may be that the feeding, weaning and toilet-training practices of our parents, and their later disciplinary practices, did not wisely condition us to endure the inevitable frustrations of life. Then we are likely to react inadequately to the annoyances, the oppositions, the disappointments which we constantly encounter. We have a low boiling point; we are hot-tempered.

Here we face an apparent dilemma. Medical opinion says that if you are angry it is better to release your anger than to keep it bottled up. Go ahead and shout and rant. Get it out of your system. If you repress it, your anger may damage your heart, cause ulcers, or find some other harmful outlet. So let yourself pop; it will be a good prophylaxis.

On the other hand God tells us that wilful anger is a sin: "Anger and fury are both of them abominable, and the sinful man shall be subject to them" (Eccl. 27:33). Our Lord Jesus is very emphatic on the subject of anger: "I say to you that everyone who is angry with his brother shall be liable to judgment" (Matt. 5:22). Here then is our dilemma: the doctors tell us to give vent to our anger, Jesus tells us that anger is a sin. Whom shall we believe?

If we had to make a choice between the two, we know well enough whom we should believe. As it happens however there is no real dilemma. The doctors are right; bottled-up anger can do us a lot of physical and mental harm. But Jesus isn't asking us to bottle up our anger; bottled-up anger still could be a sin. Jesus is telling us not to *get* angry; or, if we feel the stirrings of anger, to dissolve the anger quickly.

Why do we get angry, anyway? We get angry because we have been in some way frustrated and we can't stand frustration. It may be that our pride has been hurt, or our self-esteem. It may be that some cherished plan has been upset, or that our convenience has been interfered with, or that our wisdom has been questioned or our "rights" ignored ("Why wasn't I consulted?").

Jesus has given us the remedy: to hate the sin but to love the sinner. Spelled out, that means that when someone does us an injustice, or by thoughtlessness or stupidity hurts us, we say to ourselves, "Poor fellow (or poor woman) he must be a pretty unhappy person. He's hurting himself more than he's hurting me. He must get himself in a lot of jams with that meanness (or thoughtlessness or stupidity). I'll say a little prayer for him that God may give him the grace to change. Meanwhile I'll keep my own head cool. Getting angry isn't going to put the pieces back together."

That kind of reasoning doesn't bottle up the anger; it *evaporates* the anger before our temper slips the leash. It is hard for some persons to realize that anger is a weakness. The angry man has abandoned control of himself. He has let another person take charge of his emotions, he is letting another person (or a situation) push him around emotionally. From our own experience we know that if we can get another person angry, we feel that we have scored a victory. In an argument it makes us doubly furious if the other person refuses to get angry. He has licked us by his self-control.

The even-tempered man (or woman) is a strong person. He is lovable as a friend, thrice dangerous as an enemy. Dangerous because he is clearheaded, his reasoning powers are functioning, he is in command of himself and is not letting his emotions take over.

No matter how hot-tempered we may be "by nature," it is a weakness which we can conquer if we have the will. That is, it is a weakness which we can conquer with the grace which God will give us for the asking. It may not be an easy task and it may take a bit of time. If we have been letting our temper victimize us for years, we are unlikely to conquer it in a day. Gradually we shall develop this state of mind: "I'm sorry for him. I'll pray for him. Getting angry will accomplish nothing. And the whole thing isn't that important anyway. In the light of eternity, what difference will it make? I'm going to be boss of myself and of my own emotions. Old man Anger, hold out your hands for the manacles!"

When, with prayer and with effort, we have achieved this attitude—then we shall be master of ourselves, with no ulcer in our future.

III

Parents sometimes are troubled in conscience because they seem so easily to become angry with their children. Yet the truth is that parents who never would get angry at their children would be the ones more in danger of sinning. A parent who would view his child's misbehavior without any show of anger would be unjust to the child as well as unjust to God. The principal way in which a youngster learns to distinguish between good and evil is by the evidence of pleasure or displeasure on the part of his parents.

We are not speaking here of the parent whose anger is chronic: the rigid father who expects everyone to jump when he speaks and can brook no faintest show of independence; or the mother who always whines, always nags, always criticizes and never praises. Parents such as these are mentally sick, and it is not with such exceptions that we are here concerned.

However it does happen now and then that even a normal parent's anger may be unreasonable. If mother is tired and nervous she may scold much too harshly for some minor childish mistake. If father is absorbed in the newspaper or in some worry of his own he may bark much too roughly at the youngster who thoughtlessly interrupts him. Parents are human and parents will make mistakes. Fortunately God seems to have

57

equipped children with shock absorbers against such mistakes. A child who is conscious of being loved and who feels secure in his relationship with his parents, will survive quite nicely these occasional outbursts of unreasonable or excessive parental anger.

What parents have to realize—and most do realize —is that there are times when anger is a virtue, a virtue which parents must practice. Often children just will not awaken to the seriousness of their misconduct unless the parent shows anger. Parental anger at such a time is *just* anger, righteous anger. We might define righteous anger as that which is directed against evil actions for God's and neighbor's sake, rather than against an individual for our own sake. A parent who is angry at a disobedient child really is angry about the disobedience. The parent still loves the child and seeks only the child's good. There is no question of a grudge against the child; the anger disappears as soon as the behavior changes.

This then is the test for righteous anger: Am I angry because God's rights have been violated and the good of others has been threatened? Or am I angry simply because I personally have been offended? The former is righteous anger, the latter is quite likely to be sinful anger.

The classic example of just anger is found in our Lord's scourging of the money changers from the Temple. Jesus was not embittered against the money changers as individuals; on the contrary, He soon would die for them. His fury was against the evil institution which they represented: a device by which pilgrims from foreign lands were victimized as they exchanged their foreign currency in order to buy sacrifices for the Temple. Custom and apathetic public opinion had established the money changers as an inescapable evil. It took the awful anger of Jesus to expose the evil.

We have to remember that the passion of anger was given to us by God as a part of our human nature. Like other human passions, anger has its lawful purposes. It is needful as a means of self-preservation, a defense against unjust aggression. It also is an instrument of charity, moving us to defend the weak and the helpless. Above all it is a weapon against sin and against all institutions which propagate sin. As is the case with other human urges, anger becomes sinful only by misuse or excess.

Unfortunately original sin has disturbed the control which reason should exert over the passions. As a consequence we too often find ourselves becoming angry with each other because of personal slights, jealousies and selfish resentments. Far too seldom do we manifest the just anger which should be enkindled in us by such evils as pornographic literature made available to our children on the newsstands, dope-selling and filth sales to our high school youth, racial injustice in our own town and neighborhood, graft in government. We could do with some righteous anger

59

in such areas as these. A controlled and purposeful rage against the exploitation of the innocent and the weak is the kind of anger that would be pleasing to God.

We usually speak of anger as being a sin, simply because unjust or excessive anger is the type of anger in which the world most abounds. However it would be most unfortunate if our adrenal glands ever became so quiescent that they could not respond to the challenge of sin and injustice. It is not virtue to be complacent when God's rights and our neighbor's good are under attack.

VII

THE POWER WITHIN YOU

I

A DIAMOND may be smeared with black tar so that none of its beauty shows through. Underneath the tar the diamond still will be a gem of brilliant beauty; but if we've never seen a diamond except those smeared with tar, we're likely to have a very poor opinion of diamonds.

The procreative power is a thing of beauty too, a magnificent gift of God. However, a person whose knowledge of sex began with gutter talk in childhood and ripened on the smutty stories of the factory or office lunchroom—that person is almost certain to have a distorted view of sex and of all that pertains to it. The distorted view may have been intensified by unwise parents. In training a child to modesty, parents sometimes leave a youngster with the impression that his or her genital organs are in some way bad or nasty, an impression from which the child may never fully recover. We have seen parents go almost panicky with embarrassment because four year old Tommie wanders into the living room without his pants on; instead of picking him up with a smile and a kiss and carrying him casually back to his clothes. Parents who themselves are confused in their attitude towards sex are likely to perpetuate their attitude in their offspring.

Nothing that God has made is evil, least of all the human organs which are God's special instruments for His work of creation. A lesson in modesty should be a lesson in reverence. A child should be taught that the private parts of his body are a sacred area which belongs in a very special way to God. According to his capacity to understand, it should be explained to him that very holy things are kept covered, like the veiled tabernacle on the altar, and the chalice which the priest carries to and from the altar. Needless to say, a child's questions should be answered truthfully and without evidence of embarrassment, to the extent that will satisfy the child's present curiosity.

Further training in chastity will simply be an enlargement of this initial sense of reverence. The precious power of parenthood which God has entrusted to boys and to girls is to be cherished and safeguarded until, in holy marriage, God takes a boy and a girl to be partners with Himself. Any use of this grand gift outside of marriage is a betrayal of God's trust; it is grave irreverence, the desecration of a power which is sacred because it touches God so closely. This is the meaning of chastity.

In most other virtues it is possible to sin venially because of the slightness of the matter involved. It is a venial sin to steal a penny, it is a venial sin to tell a harmless lie. Against the virtue of chastity however there is no "slight matter." Any conscious and deliberate excitation of the sex power outside of marriage is a grave sin. The unchaste touches and embraces which are euphemistically called "heavy necking" and "petting" are as grievously sinful as is coitus on the part of those who have not yet, in marriage, formed their partnership with God.

Even *within* marriage God's rights must be scrupulously observed. If husband and wife exercise their procreative power and at the same time interpose a positive barrier to God's creative action—that is, freeze God out of the partnership as by the use of contraceptives—then they become guilty of mortal sin. "God, You keep out of this," they say by implication. There is here also an implied sin against the virtue of hope, a lack of trust in God. "We can't afford another baby," or "My health won't stand it," is the proffered excuse. And God, Who knows perfectly the problem and Who alone knows the best answer, is shoved rudely aside.

The reason why all deliberate sins against chastity are mortal sins is because of the tremendous importance of the sexual faculty for the welfare of the human race. If the town in the valley draws its water supply from a spring on the mountainside, the city fathers will fence the spring in against vagrant animals and careless picnickers and will post prominent "Keep Out" signs.

63

Because, if the spring is polluted, the whole town will suffer.

The good of humanity depends upon the right use of the procreative power; it is the source and well-spring of life. That is why God has erected around the sexual faculty the strong barrier of marriage, and in the sixth and ninth commandments has posted His "No Trespassing" notices. In His infinite goodness God has designed to make us male and female, has deigned to make us sharers in His own creative power. But it must be on God's terms. God cannot remain indifferent if His precious gift is degraded to a plaything and the power of parenthood made a pastime.

II

There is no gainsaying that the practice of the virtue of chastity poses for many people, married and unmarried, a problem in Christian living. This is not surprising. After the instinct for survival, the sex instinct is the strongest of all the human drives. Because of its very strength it is the most difficult to discipline. There is a reason for the strength of these basic drives of ours. God gave them to us so that His purposes might be accomplished.

God endowed us with the instinct for survival or self-preservation because God wanted to insure that we as individuals would live our allotted span and would not expose our lives and health to unnecessary danger. Within its proper bounds this instinct works well; we eat when we need food, we look carefully before we cross a busy street, we consult a doctor when we feel pain. Under stress however this instinct can make sorry spectacles of us. In panic people will trample one another to death trying to save their own lives; in famine people will fight and even kill one another for a scrap of food; under torture people will betray their friends to escape with their own skins. That is, they will do these things unless they have learned to discipline self, unless they hold to other values that are higher than mere survival.

Besides the instinct for self-preservation God has bestowed upon humans the instinct for preservation of the race—the sex instinct. For the working out of God's plan it is necessary not only that the individual should take care of his life; it is necessary also that the human race should perpetuate itself, begetting the successors to whom it may entrust its stewardship of the created universe. Because the perpetuation of the race is of such importance to His plan, God has attached to the exercise of the sexual power a high degree of physical pleasure. Just as God has annexed pleasure to the act of eating so that we may not die of malnutrition through lack of interest in food, so also has God joined an even keener physical pleasure to the act of procreation so that the human race may not perish through lack of incitement to parenthood.

We have noted that the drive for personal survival

can degrade us if it is allowed to operate beyond its proper limits; if for example we cling to life at the cost of our humanity, or, on a lower plane, if we make the pleasure of eating an end in itself and sin by gluttony. The sex drive likewise can debase us if it is exercised without regard for the purposes or the bounds established by God. What are those purposes? What are those bounds?

In planning the human race God did a most gracious thing. He chose to make mankind partners with Him in His work of creation; partners in the very highest of His works of physical creation: in the fashioning of human life. God did not have to create us male and female. He could have provided for the perpetuation of the human race in many other ways. He could have made us a sexless race of beings, Himself creating each body individually as He does now create each soul individually.

In His infinite goodness, however, God did choose to share with us His own creative power. Man, woman and God; these three would be partners. By an act of profound love which would express the complete giving of themselves to one another, man and woman would initiate the new human body into which God would infuse the new spiritual soul. This would be parenthood, in which the paternal strength and providence of God and the maternal tenderness and patience of God would be reflected by diffraction in human mother and father.

66

The dignity of parenthood is enhanced by a further privilege accorded by God. Father and mother are not only to be partners of God in the creation of new human life, they also are to be His partners in the nurturing of the child's spiritual soul. Parents not only will be the procreators of children, they also will be the makers and the molders of saints. Under the warmth of their love for each other and for the child, this new soul will unfold and flower with the sanctity willed for it by God. Through the love of his parents for him, the child will learn what it means to be loved by God; through his own love for his parents the child will learn what it means to love the God Who gave them to him. Through the prayers and the example of the parents, God will channel His graces to the child. Not merely to people the earth with humans, but to people heaven with saints: this is the ultimate meaning of parenthood.

The sexual drive underlies all this and is a part of the total gift of marital love and (when God so wills) parenthood. Original sin destroyed the perfect control which reason was to have exerted over it, as over other human drives. But no amount of misuse and abuse can destroy the beauty and the holiness of God's gift of sex.

VIII

THE WAY YOU GO

I

TO THE OLD ADAGE, "Love is blind," may be traced most unhappy marriages. There are exceptional instances in which a person, due to mental illness, undergoes after marriage a radical personality change which could not have been foreseen. Aside from such exceptional cases, a person's basic personality is firmly fixed by the time he or she comes to marriageable age. In a courtship of any reasonable length that basic personality can be recognized by the other party in the courtship—if he or she has open eyes.

Unfortunately love—or let us say physical infatuation—is a great eye closer and a great rationalizer. "I know he drinks a little," (he is tipsy on half their dates), "but that's just because he's so shy; he'll be all right once we're married." "Sure she's kind of bossy, but she's such a sweet kid you don't mind that; and once we're married I'll wear the pants." "He does fly into a temper about such little things and it seems we're always quarreling; but he's nervous and high strung. Marriage will change that." "Gosh she's jealous! I can hardly kiss my own sister. But I suppose she's afraid she might lose me; after we're married she'll be different."

We all have heard wishful thinking such as this. Sometimes it is because physical desire has put reason to sleep. Sometimes it is because the defender is so anxious to get married that he or she will settle for almost any kind of partner who comes along. Then too there are the pathological cases: the mother-dominated son who unconsciously seeks a wife who will dominate him; the girl who is driven by unrecognized guilt feelings to choose a brutal husband who will provide the punishment she unconsciously craves.

Original sin has disturbed the control that reason should exert over the biological urge, so perhaps it is not too surprising that many young men and women walk blindly into a marriage foredoomed to unhappiness; walk into it in spite of the danger signals that were flying full mast for any intelligent person to see. The alcoholic husbands, the nagging wives, the vicious-tempered men and the insanely jealous women: these didn't suddenly develop their undesirable traits after marriage. And the naive belief that, "I can get him (or her) to change," flies in the face of all the psychological evidence—the evidence that a person's basic personality pattern does not change after maturity. A person may grow in virtue with the years, but deep-seated emotional and psychological disorders usually will grow worse; barring a miracle, of course—and few miracles of this kind occur.

Fortunately those who see marriage as a vocation (and thank God their number is legion) do retain some vestiges of discrimination and do try to make a wise and a prayerful choice. They not only ask, "Will he (or she) and I have fun together?" They also ask, "Will he make a good father (or she a good mother) to my children?"

However, even in the great multitude of normally happy marriages there sometimes are areas of stress which result from the mistaken idea that another person can change his personality at our command. An important ingredient of happiness in marriage is the willingness to accept each other "as we are." The perfect match is a rare phenomenon. Almost inevitably there will be personality differences, clashes of temperament. The need is to adjust to these differences, rather than to expect to change them.

If a wife is by nature a poor manager, no amount of griping is going to make her a smart budgeter and an efficient housekeeper. It will be a happier marriage if the husband will accept and love her as she is, and quietly do his best to make up for her deficiencies (as she almost certainly is making up for his). If a husband is by nature a quiet, stay-at-home sort of person, no amount of complaining is going to change him into a party-going, crowd-loving individual. A vivacious wife may find this a trial, but it will be a happier marriage if she cheerfully accepts the fact and stops trying to make the man over. The wife may be an inordinate-

70

ly neat individual who can't stand the sight of a pin out of place, and the husband a sloppy fellow who never puts things away. The man may be an obsessively punctual person who wants everything on the dot, and the wife a fluttery person who never has dinner on time.

"You have your faults and I have mine. Let's just accept each other as we are. Let's be willing to settle for the good that we find in each other (and *look* for the good) so that under God ours may be a happy marriage and a happy home." That is a simple and yet an infallible philosophy upon which to build a day-by-day satisfying marriage. Blessed will be the children who grow up in the peace and the charity of such a home.

II

Today as I passed a Chinese laundry I noticed a sign in the window: "Complete bachelor service; washing, ironing, mending, darning." The sign started a train of thought in my mind. I pictured the bachelor on his way to the coffee shop for breakfast, dropping his bundle off for the ministration of impersonal fingers; then calling for his bundle on his way home in the evening, his mind busy planning some activity for the night that will keep him from feeling the loneliness that seems to be exuded by the walls of his furnished room or apartment. Then my thoughts swung to a con-

trasting picture: the husband, breathless from his romp
with the youngsters who have just gone to bed, switch-
ing on the TV as his wife settles in another chair with
the shirt that needs a button and the socks that need a
bit of yarn.

Probably there are few husbands and wives who
have not, during some period of exceptional stress, felt
stirrings of envy for the "carefree" life of some unmarried friend or acquaintance. To be able to go and
come as one pleases, to have nobody to worry about
and no one to answer to except oneself: ah (says the
tempter) what a life! Guiltily the spouse wonders
whether he or she would ever get married if he or she
had a chance to do it over again. Then the mood
passes and the sky brightens—and anyway it's too late
to turn back now.

No marriage can sustain the high plateau of surging
happiness all the time. There are bound to be some
dips, some valleys. Children's illnesses, financial crises,
physical and mental fatigue that make a person irritable
and over-sensitive, work-worries and sleepless nights
and even a touch of constipation—these are the things
that can make us feel misunderstood and unappre-
ciated, and what marriage can escape them entirely?
It is then that the grass looks so much greener on the
other side of the matrimonial fence.

The spouse who finds himself in an emotional slump
would do well to remember that the advantages of
"single blessedness" exists mostly in the imagination of

the married person himself. The bachelor and the spinster (horrid word!) are free to go and come, yes. They are free to go and come because nobody gives much of a darn whether they *do* go or come. Probably the greatest cross in the life of a single person is the lack of somebody who is really one's own, the feeling that if he dropped out of sight tomorrow, no one would greatly care.

The loneliness of the single can be temporarily smothered in the company of friends and in the excitement of artificial amusements: the theater, the night club, the cocktail party, the poker game. But in terms of solid happiness the freedom of the bachelor girl at the cocktail party is far outranked by the bondage of the woman who shares a midnight snack with her husband at the kitchen table. In terms of genuine joy-giving, the cleverest nightclub performer cannot be compared to a baby who has just discovered his toes—when the baby is your own. And on the scale of human satisfaction, a hundred friends will be outweighed by one wife, or one husband.

Some persons remain single by necessity of duty, duty to an aged parent perhaps, or to younger brothers and sisters. Some persons remain single because they honestly feel that a single life in the world is their true vocation, and the world owes much to the selfish service of such dedicated souls. (We are not talking here of priests and religious who have found deep satisfaction and happiness in the spiritual fatherhood and

73

motherhood to which God has called them.) Some persons remain single because subconsciously they are afraid of marriage and never seem to find the "right man" or the "right woman"—precisely because they have set up, as a defense against their fear, an impossible standard which no man or woman could meet. Finally there are the few who remain single because of their constitutional selfishness, who offer incense only to themselves, who cannot bring themselves to share with another anything of significant value, much less to share themselves. These are the ones who brag of the joys of freedom and who discover, too late, the ashes of their freedom in their lonely hands.

It is well that these last ones do stay single, because marriage is above all else a sharing—with each other and with God. The great bulk of the unhappy marriages are those in which one or both of the parties cannot or will not share.

This has been quite a bit of philosophizing to stem from just a sign in a laundry window. The truths which we have recalled are obvious and familiar, yet are too easily lost sight of in those moments when the golden yoke of marriage seems to rub and pinch.

In a restaurant not long ago I sat near a group of women, thirtyish or so and apparently from the same office. It seemed to be a birthday party for one of the group and they all were quite hilarious. Then a young couple came in, and with their three small children took a table nearby. The hilarity tapered off as most of the eyes at the birthday table stole glances at the new arrivals. I caught a remark or two: "Isn't she the sweetest little thing? Look at those curls!" and "Isn't the baby a doll? Look at those chubby cheeks!" For a few moments the party was somewhat subdued, as though each was busy with her own thoughts. If they had dared speak those thoughts aloud I am sure most would have said, "You lucky married people!"

III

Some times we use the word "vocation" to refer to the kind of work we do: mechanic, teacher, merchant or whatever our calling may be. More strictly however the word "vocation" designates the particular state in life which a person embraces. Broadly there are two such vocations: the vocation to marriage and the vocation to the celibate life. The celibate life has what we might call "sub-vocations": the priesthood, the religious state, membership in a secular institute, and a single life in the world. It is of this last mentioned vocation, a single life in the world, that we would like to speak here.

God has made the human race male and female, and has placed in each individual a strong feeling of attraction to the opposite sex. God wills that man and woman should complement each other, spiritually and psychologically as well as emotionally and physically. In finding fulfillment in each other, man and woman at the same time are instruments of God's creative power. They are God's partners in populating earth and heaven. This is what we may term God's grand master-plan.

However every master plan provides for special circumstances and needs. God's master plan is no exception. There is work to be done that can best be done—and sometimes only can be done—by persons who are unimpeded by marital or family ties. Sometimes it is a personal work, such as the care of sick or aged parents. Sometimes it is a work of more extended charity such as nursing or social service, or some other career that calls for exceptional self-dedication. Objectively it might appear that certain persons could just as well be married as far as their work is concerned. Yet, abstracting from the person who remains unmarried through mere selfishness, we may be sure that the single person does have a particular part in God's design. It sometimes is a part that may be hidden from his or her own eyes as well as from ours.

How can a person tell whether or not he or she has a vocation to the single life in the world? First we might note one misconception concerning vocations which we frequently encounter. This is the mistaken idea that God normally calls us by some sensible sign to the life or the work which He wants us to do. We feel that God ought in some way to let us see His beckoning finger. Yet that is not God's ordinary way of doing things.

God seldom does by supernatural means what he can accomplish through natural means. God is a great believer in using what already is at hand. He steers us by the circumstances of life around us more often than by a direct illumination of our minds. There is many a good priest in the Church today who first went to the seminary mostly because he liked and admired the priest who suggested that he do so. Many a good religious is in the convent because she fancied herself in a religious habit or thought that the convent would be such a peaceful and carefree life. Motives like these will be purified as time goes on. Meantime why should God send a messenger from heaven to extend His call when He can give us a push in a hundred different ways, through the people and the circumstances around us? So, the angels may be chuckling at the single girl who thinks she is unmarried just because no one ever proposed; the angels know who cut off the proposals. And the man who thinks it was his sick mother who kept him single may one day discover that his mother's illness was a handy tool for God to use.

The single life does present exceptional problems, and for that reason it can be a dangerous choice for a person who embraces celibacy for selfish reasons. God does not still by a miracle the surging of sexual passion in the man or woman who follows the single vocation, nor does God eliminate in them the parental instinct. What God does do is to give needed extra graces to those of good will, to those who make full use of prayer and the sacraments. With God's grace they are able to control the sexual urge, redirecting and utilizing this elemental force as a powerful drive in the selfless service to which the single person so often is dedicated. This process of rechanneling the procreative power into fields of service other than the family is termed "sublimation" by the psychologists. Sublimating is a far cry from frustration. There may be "frustrated old maids" and "frustrated bachelors," but they will not be found among the God-motivated adherents to the single life.

A celibate life in the world is perhaps the most difficult of all vocations. It is far from easy to live holily and happily with none of the supports of family life or religious community. For that very reason, those whom God has guided to the single vocation will find it a life abundant in grace and merit. It is their divinely appointed path to heaven.

IX

THE WAY YOU WORK

I

CALLING UPON His infinite wisdom and power, God brought the universe into existence. He created the universe, we might say, in its "raw" state. Having started things off, God has entrusted to His creature Man the task of continuing God's creative work. Out of the raw materials which God has provided and with the talents that God has given, mankind must labor towards the final fulfillment of the plan which God has in mind.

From ancient man's invention of the wheel to modern man's splitting of the atom; from ancient man's discovery of copper and bronze to modern man's development of alloy steel; from ancient man's invention of geometry to modern man's fashioning of an electronic brain—man labors under God to complete the work of creation. There are detours of course and there are retreats. New discoveries may be used for evil as well as for good. But God's hand will not be stayed, and creation moves on.

The contribution of any single individual usually

is a tiny one. Even the great inventions most often
are the work of many; of many brains and hands working together, or of one building upon what another
previously has done. The work of some is directly
creative: that of the miner who mines the ore, of the
operator who rolls the sheets of steel, of the assembler
who fastens the body to the chassis of the new car.
The work of others is re-creative: that of the doctor
who mends bodies, of the dry cleaner who refurbishes
clothes, of the mechanic who re-bores the engine.

Some work with physical matter, as do plumbers
and candymakers, and foremen and board chairmen
by remote control. Others work with minds and souls,
as do parents and priests and teachers, artists and en-
tertainers. Each in his own way is making his own
contribution. And, since only God knows what His
final plan is, none of us can rightly say that this person's
task is more important than that person's. Human
methods of measuring results are not necessarily God's.
Of this only can we be sure: that unless our work is
positively destructive (and we are not talking of the
re-creative work of housewreckers) or unless our work
is an obvious waste of time and energy—then we are
doing God's work, whether we know it or not.

It is too bad if we do not know it. It is the curse
of too many people today that they do not know it,
or do not think of it. They see their jobs only as distasteful burdens imposed by the necessity of "earn-
ing a living." They do not see themselves as God's

80

creative instruments, God's agents. And if a man (or a woman) cannot see that, then there can be no deep satisfaction, no real happiness in what he does, even if it is the construction of an Empire State building, or the writing of a best seller.

It is the sense of a divine purposefulness behind our labors that makes for a Christian philosophy of work. Without that sense of purposefulness, the biggest job in the world can seem like a blind-alley job. A Christian approach to work does not necessarily mean that we shall enjoy work. By their nature some tasks are more interesting and therefore more enjoyable than others. But aside from the seeming dreariness of some tasks, original sin has made all work to some degree a penance. (Even if Adam had not sinned we still would work, but all work would be play.) Yet the fact of original sin need not make work an unrelieved pain. There still is joy to be found in work, even in the drearier tasks, when we are conscious of the truth that we are members of God & Company, that we and God are in this together.

There are a couple of conclusions that flow from this fact of our partnership with God. One such conclusion is that we should endeavor to make the best possible use of our talents, all circumstances considered. It is this sense of responsibility to God that will steer us safely between sloth on the one hand and overweening ambition on the other. Sloth might tempt us to stay on a job that is easy and without responsibility, rather than to take on a job (perhaps even at lesser pay) where our God-given talents could be used more effectively or over a wider field. It is not necessarily humility to say, "I'm satisfied where I am," if there is greater good we could do higher up. Ambition might lead us to seek more money or greater power for their own sake, regardless of what God's will might be, regardless of primary duties to family or to others.

A Christian philosophy of work also will inspire us to give our best to our job, however humble the job may be. We shall be honest in our work (watch the water-cooler and the restroom!) and conscientious about our work; not to please any boss or board of directors, but solely because it is God's work that we are doing, and God's work must not be done otherwise than well.

II

What have you read lately? If you were to meet one of your former teachers, and he or she were to ask you that question, would you feel embarrassed as you gave your answer?

We know that a factory which habitually operated at ten percent of capacity would soon be in bankruptcy. Yet a respected psychologist has said that most people go to their graves without having used more than ten percent of their mental capacity. This seems a shocking statement. The brain which God has given us is a marvelous instrument, with almost limitless possibilities for absorbing knowledge, for enjoying and using knowledge. We believe that God will one day demand an accounting for the gifts which He has entrusted to us. It is a sobering thought to contemplate that we may be using only ten percent of our intellectual potential.

If our mental fare is confined to TV, newspapers, and light magazine or novel reading, we have reason for concern. These things in moderation have their place. To live in the world we have to know something of what is going on in the world. And even the keenest brain will function better with occasional relaxation and catharsis. But to let our brain waste its energies habitually on trivialities surely was not God's purpose in designing this tool of thought.

Even aside from our Christian responsibility to use our great gift of mind, there is the added consideration that an unexercised mind grows old more quickly. If we content ourselves with soaking up mere information and emotions from newspapers, television, and popular magazines, without any solid exercise of the mind in the form of thought and reasoning, then we are aging faster than we realize. It is not the soundness of wind and limb, but the alertness of the mind that is the true measure of age. Some people do keep their minds active and vigorous with a fairly steady diet of serious reading. They are familiar with the non-fiction shelves of their local public library and their library card is in frequent use. Such persons however may still underfeed their intellects if their reading is confined to secular works. The mind of a Christian ought to be a *Christian* mind, seeing life and life's problems from the viewpoint of Christ. Christ's viewpoint seldom is that of secular writers; and it will not be our viewpoint if secular writers are our only guide.

Our aim must be to grow not only in practical knowledge but to grow also in grace, to feed the soul as well as the inquiring mind. Often the two objectives can be combined, as when parents read a book like Burns' *Mental Health in Childhood*, or an engaged couple read a book like Keenan & Ryan's *Marriage: A Medical and Sacramental Study*, or any one of us reads a book like Royce's *Personality and Mental Health*.

Nevertheless in addition to practical knowledge our minds must have the insight to make truly Christian judgments, since we encounter so many problems which we must face and solve for ourselves. Here we shall be helped by such books as Sheed's *Theology for Beginners* or *Theology and Sanity;* by such books as Riccioti's *Life of Christ* or Charles' *Prayer for All Time;* by such books as Howell's *Of Sacraments and Sacrifice* or Bouyer's *Liturgical Piety.* We cannot think in the pattern of Christ unless we have given our minds the food for such thoughts by means of systematic spiritual reading.

Far too many Catholics are quite unaware of the

wealth of stimulating reading that can be found on the shelves of any Catholic bookstore or lending library. And, aware or unaware, there is always the excuse that we are too busy. "I know I should do more serious reading," we admit, "and I'd like to; but when shall I ever find the time?"

One way in which to find the time would be to count up all the minutes in any average day which are spent on newspapers, secular magazines and TV (or just puttering around). It may not be a lot, but it will be something. Then let us slice off just twenty-five percent of that time for worthwhile reading. We may find to our surprise that we can read and digest one soul-building book each week. If that strikes us as too rich a diet, we at least could begin with one such book a month.

The truth is that all too often we just do not have the initiative to get started. We quiet our conscience by telling ourselves that we shall get around to it next week or next month. We do not commit ourselves by reaching *now* for the phone (or for a pen) to make contact with a Catholic bookstore or lending library. Then, when that first step is taken, we face another obstacle: after being so long fed on the cooked cereal of light reading, our mind rebels after the first page or two of a serious book—and the book remains unread.

If we could but get ourselves over these initial obstacles, we should find it an exhilarating experience to awaken some part of those nine-tenths of unused brain cells; brain cells which have done no work since we were born and which otherwise may go with us, unused, to the grave.

X

THE WAY YOU LIVE

I

IT IS EASY to become the slave of *things*. Man's instinct for ownership is a good instinct, a part of the human nature which God has made. Man's right to private ownership, his right to possess whatever may be necessary for his spiritual and temporal welfare, is a right that the Church has defended through the centuries. If the right of ownership were not a good impulse, its free renunciation by the vow of poverty would not be the highly meritorious act that it is.

However, the spiritual palsy which is the result of original sin makes it difficult for us to control our naturally good desires and instincts. The palsy victim may reach for something and find, because of his lack of muscular coordination, that he has reached too far or too short. Similarly do we often find difficulty in holding to their God-intended purposes the natural drives with which God has endowed us. It is so easy for us to lose control, so easy for us to go to extremes.

That is why our instinct for ownership often gets out of hand and becomes the vice of covetousness. Probably none of us is threatened with the gross kind

87

of covetousness which seeks to acquire at the expense of others; the kind of covetousness which leads to embezzlement, fraud and other types of injustice. But there is another species of covetousness which is more insidious even though it is less grievous: it is the inordinate seeking of temporal goods by loving or desiring them too much. To this sort of covetousness almost all of us are exposed; against it all of us have to be on our guard.

This intemperate acquisitiveness may not lead to conduct that is criminal, but it often does result in grave injustice to others. There is the father, for example, who is so wrapped up in making money that his wife and children seldom see him. He will say that he is working so hard for the sake of his family, when in reality he loves the money or what the money will buy. If he asked his family he would find that they would much rather see more of himself and do with less money. The situation is greatly aggravated when the mother of the family also works outside the home. She will say, "With the extra paycheck I can do so much more for the children," when in reality she loves the feeling of independence that her paycheck gives. And if she brought home a million extra dollars it never could make up to the children for the happiness and the security which they lose because of her unnecessary absence from the home.

The devil doesn't have to work very hard to lure us to covetousness; not as long as he has a great part of the advertising industry working on his side. Beautiful full-color ads tempt us with labor-saving devices and gadgets from all the magazine pages, and the black-and-white ads of the newspapers complement the color ads by telling us what a bargain it will be if we buy it today.

A true-life incident will illustrate the absurdities to which covetousness can lead. Two men live side by side on sixty foot lots. One man has a fifteen dollar hand mower and mows his lawn nicely in an hour. The other man has a sixty dollar power mower and, counting the time he tinkers with the motor, averages two hours for each cutting. Yet the first man plans to buy a power mower next payday, and the second man is planning to trade his present mower in on a more expensive, self-propelled model—with more tinkering-time a certainty.

Once we let covetousness take hold of us, we never are satisfied, no matter what we have got. Covetousness feeds upon pride, and someone else always has something that we haven't yet got, or there is a newer model that makes us dissatisfied with the old. Just page through the ads: "No more wash-day blues," "Greater ease of handling," "New upswept beauty," "TV with a clarity of picture you've never known," and all the other sweet siren songs. Why should the devil bother working?

Once covetousness gets hold of us we have a thirst like that of the shipwrecked sailor. The more salt water he drinks the thirstier the sailor gets. The more things the covetous person acquires, the more he must have.

The antidote to covetousness is the spirit of detachment, which basically means to have a true sense of proportion, a true sense of values—spiritual values as well as marketplace values, human values as well as physical values. The detached man is never a slave to things. He is content to have what he needs and high-powered ads leave his pulse unquickened. Even from what he already has he could walk away in a minute if his duty to God or to neighbor made it desirable. His is the family whose members find their greatest joy in each other rather than in an abundance of merchandise, and extra income is not prized more highly than the integrity of the home. True detachment is harder to acquire than it might seem—but prayer and honest thinking can achieve it.

II

One of the best-hidden yet most dangerous obstacles to the living of a fully Christian life is the half pagan atmosphere in which we live. Here in America we treat God much as we treat an ex-President: with the deference due to a once powerful figure who no longer really counts for much. We listen to his views with interest but without feeling any compulsion to act upon what he says. God seldom is denied outright; rather is He simply ignored in the political, the economical and the social life of our nation. God swings no more weight than if He lived in Independence or Palo Alto.

This attitude towards God is what we call the spirit of secularism. Religion is good, says secularism; it is good to go to church on Sunday; it is good to pray. But when it comes to the business of living we have to be practical. When policies are to be formed and decisions made, the only question that matters is: What will best work out to our advantage? Secularism would laugh at the idea of trying to look at things from God's viewpoint; that sort of thinking is strictly for visionaries. Keep religion in the church where it belongs.

Day after day we live and breathe in this atmosphere of expediency. It is not surprising if our souls become infected. It is not surprising if we encounter individuals who go on thinking of themselves as "practical Catholics" when actually their Catholicity has been relegated long since to Sunday mornings only.

Here for example is a woman who is seen regularly at the Communion rail. "Of course," she confides to a friend, "I don't tell in confession that I use contraceptives. I figure that's my business, no matter what the Church says." The poor soul does not even realize that her faith is all but dead and that her religious practices are a hollow shell without substance. Because, if she does not believe that the Church speaks for God in interpreting His law, then she does not really believe in the Church at all. She is totally illogical in believing in confession and in Holy Communion, since it is the

91

same Church which, in Christ's name, vouches for the reality of these. Secularism ("Keep religion in its place") has claimed another victim.

There are so many examples of this secularistic contamination, this kind of twisted thinking. There are the Catholic parents who will dismiss the Church's teaching on the matter of steady dating. "I can't see that there's any harm in it. I can trust my kids. And anyway all the other high school youngsters are doing it." There are the Catholics in business (or in politics or in the professions) who will shrug off a bit of sharp practice: "I know the Church says it's wrong, but I have to face facts if I want to make a living. Everybody else does it; I've got to do it."

There is the Catholic young person who says, "The Church is too old fashioned; I just can't see that a little petting is so very wrong." There is the segregationist Catholic who says, "It's all very well to talk about racial justice, but the Pope doesn't have to live with these people like I do." There is the Catholic mother-in-law who says, "Of course I know it's wrong for a divorced man to remarry, but after all those children do need a mother." There is the Catholic sophisticate who says, "Sure it's a Class C picture but it can't do me any harm; and I'm old enough to judge for myself."

None of these speakers would dare to come out flatly and say, "I believe in doing right as long as it is reasonably easy, but not when it starts to hurt." The martyrs through the ages would face them down on that, particularly today's martyrs behind the Iron Curtain. Neither would the speakers dare to go all the way and say, "I just simply do not agree with God." Always they try to make an imaginary distinction between Christ and His Church, and so doing blind themselves to their own inconsistency. If the Church is not Christ's mouthpiece, why believe anything? Christ will not allow us to drive a wedge between Him and His Bride. We cannot bypass the Church and expect to find Christ on the other side.

These examples which we have quoted are of course some of the more extreme instances of the way in which the polluted air of secularism can infiltrate and infect our own spirit. We ourselves may not have gone so far but we need, all of us, occasionally to take our own spiritual temperature and to diagnose the degree of our infection. Blessed indeed are we if we have schooled ourselves to think with Christ and His Church, if we have trained ourselves to live by principle in little things as well as big.

This will mean that we live in God's presence every day wherever we are, not just in church on Sundays. It will mean that "what God would want me to do" is the basic ingredient of all our decisions. It will mean that we have recognized that Christ and His Mystical Body are indivisible and that it is His voice which speaks through His Church. With God's grace we *can* live in a secularistic world without being infected —but it is a grace to be prayed for.

XI

THE WAY YOU LOVE

I

"How can I possibly love that woman next door? She yells at my children if they so much as step off the sidewalk in front of her house. The only time I ever tried to borrow something from her, she said she didn't have any sugar to loan and slammed the door in my face. The night we had that perfectly innocent birthday party for my son, she complained to the police that we were having a drunken brawl. How can I ever love that woman? I feel more like wringing her neck."

If we never have talked this way about some other person, the chances are that we at least have been tempted to similar thoughts. It may be a neighbor, it may be the boss, it may be a fellow-worker, it may be a relative. It even may be someone we have not seen, perhaps a criminal of whose fiendish deeds we have read in the newspapers.

Sometimes too we meet up with *good* people who seem hard to love. These are the people who seem to have a knack for rubbing us the wrong way, people whose mere presence seems to irritate us, people with whom we never see eye to eye. This natural antipathy of person for person, even of good person for good person, is the inevitable result of differences of character, differences of taste.

Almost certainly there is someone in our past or present whom we find it difficult to love. Yet we *must* love our neighbor. After giving us His first great commandment of love for God, Jesus continues, "And the second is like to it, 'Thou shalt love thy neighbor as thyself.' On these two commandments depend the whole Law and the Prophets" (Matt. 22:38). Jesus made it very plain, too, that He is not talking merely of our "nice" neighbors: "You have heard that it was said, 'Thou shalt love thy neighbor, and shalt hate thy enemy.' But I say to you, love your enemies, do good to those who persecute and calumniate you, so that you may be children of your Father in heaven. . . . For if you love those who love you, what reward shall you have? Do not even the publicans do that? And if you salute your brethren only, what are you doing more than others? Do not even the Gentiles do that?" (Matt. 5:43-47). There is no mistaking the definiteness of Jesus' command; either we love our neighbor or we are not Christ's own.

This then is the good Christian's dilemma: we must love our neighbor, yet we keep encountering people who, by any human standard, are completely unlovable. It would be a dilemma of discouraging proportions if God had not given us a special talent for loving. In the sacrament of Baptism God infused into our soul the virtue of charity, a power for loving which far surpasses any merely human facility for love. With the virtue of charity we can do supernaturally what we never could do naturally. When we are faced with a person who puts an impossible strain upon our capacity to love, the virtue of charity comes into operation. Supposing good will on our part, God will give us specific graces to enable us to surmount our natural revulsion.

Like our love for God, supernatural love for neighbor is not something that we have to feel emotionally. Supernatural love for neighbor inheres in the will rather than in the emotions. On a purely natural level we may experience a strong feeling of distaste for another person, and still have supernatural love for him. The essence of love for neighbor consists in wanting for him what God wants for him: a virtuous life here and heaven hereafter.

The practice of this love demands that we distinguish a person's malicious or revolting actions, and the person's essential self as a soul created, redeemed, and loved by God. Here again it is a matter of loving the sinner even though we must hate his sin; of condemning evil without condemning him who does the evil.

It is very easy for us to test our supernatural love for our neighbor. If someone has hurt me or has hurt someone whom I love; or if someone has a particularly obnoxious personality and makes himself thoroughly unlikeable—then let me ask myself: Do I want to see this person save his soul and get to heaven? Will I pray for this person, especially for his spiritual welfare, and repeat my prayer for him each time I find myself tempted to despise him? If he here and now were in need, perhaps perishing of hunger or injured in an accident, would I do all that I could to help him, even though he might show no gratitude for my efforts? If I can answer such questions as these with a sincere "yes," then I have at least the minimum degree of love for neighbor which Jesus demands of us all. Remembering always that it is for Jesus that I show this love, because this person, so unlovable to me, is a soul for whom Jesus died. Loving him, I love Jesus.

Hatred is the specialty of the devil. There is nothing that will bring us into closer fellowship with the devil than the sin of hatred. And conversely there is nothing that will bring us closer to Christ than love for those who are hardest to love.

II

For thousands of years God has been telling us to love our neighbor as we love ourselves, and promising eternal life to those who will do so out of their love for Him. Many people have taken God at His word, and have found that love for neighbor can make for greater happiness in this life as well as lead to the happiness of heaven.

However, it wasn't until the psychologists came along and put a dollar sign on love for neighbor, that this virtue became popular. It was discovered that "being nice to people" could pay handsome dividends. Books like Dale Carnegie's *How to Win Friends and Influence People* became the new bibles of business and society. Heaven is a long way off; but a better job or more sales or social acceptance: these are things a person can sink his teeth into right here and now. It seems that God was right, after all; and so courtesy and kindliness have become fashionable.

This is not said in a spirit of cynicism. We are grateful for any motive that will lead to greater brotherliness and harmony between man and man. Even with the psychologists to back God up, the practice of fraternal charity still is far from universal. And besides showing us that fraternal charity pays, the psychologists have done us a real service in showing us the roots of our own cussedness in this matter of neighborly love.

They have shown that the man who comes home and raises hell with his family, really is mad at his boss; against his loved ones he vents the spleen that he dare not discharge against the boss. The malicious gossiper is defending herself against the threat of her own barely-repressed passions, by proving to herself that the rest of the world is much worse than she. The fault-finder is compensating for his own unconscious feeling of inferiority by pointing to the shortcomings of others. The griper hides from himself his sense of failure and inadequacy by inferring that everybody and everything else is working against him. The hot-head is suffering from a childhood failure to develop the inner controls which would enable him to tolerate frustration.

These are some of the hidden motives which the psychologists expose for us. But we need no psychologist to tell us that a great amount of our personal unhappiness stems from our failure to get along with people better than we do—our failures in the practice of fraternal charity. Our disagreements and our dislikes, our resentments and our enmities—nothing can embitter a soul and corrode a soul as these can.

We all want to be liked by others, to be esteemed as a person worth knowing and valued as a friend worth having. We do so want to be loved by our family, cherished by our friends, liked by our neighbors, by our boss and our fellow workers; and it is so hard for us to admit that when we fail in any of these relationships, the cause lies within ourselves.

Will you perform a little experiment? Before you read beyond the end of this sentence, will you take a sheet of paper and a pencil and write down the qualities that a person ought to have in order to be loved by everybody.

Now would your own description read something like this: He (or she) is a thoroughly *kind* person, with great tolerance for the ignorance and weakness of others, being conscious of his own. He is strong in his own principles and is quick to recognize sin; but for the sinner he has only compassion and prays for him rather than condemns. He is quick to forgive injuries against himself, whether pardon is asked or not. He has great patience; does not flare up when his toes are stepped on, does not become irritated with another's mistakes. He is uniformly cheerful, and does not make others share in his headaches and his stomach upsets. He is thoughtful of the comfort and convenience of others; quick to see opportunities where he can do a kindness or lend a helping hand. He respects confidences; a secret always is safe with him. He respects reputations; if someone has done wrong, you will not hear about it from him.

The list could be lengthened, but perhaps it already is long enough to provide us with ample material for self-examination. If we are at all unhappy about our own relationships with other people, perhaps we can find the reason here. When our relationship with another person breaks down, too often we insist on pinning the blame to him, and stubbornly refuse to look in our own mirror.

As we set about the task of becoming the sort of person whom we have described—the irresistibly lovable person we all should like to be—we will not let the psychologists mislead us. They do well to point out to us the hidden motives of our behavior, but we shall greatly err if we think that these ignoble motives cannot be minimized and conquered with the grace that God will give—if we want it, if we are willing to labor at the task.

III

Perhaps we do not much care whether or not people like us. However God cares. God has a big stake in us. As members of the Mystical Body of His Son, God has empowered us by Baptism and Confirmation to be His ambassadors to the people around us. Humanly speaking God has to depend upon us to reach certain souls whom He cannot reach in any other way. We are the channels through whom God's grace must flow to others. It is our eyes and ears and mouth and hands that Jesus must use to continue His work of redemption in the world.

God *wants* us to be liked, so that we may be more effective instruments in His hands. It is only as people love us—and see us as loving them—that we can gain entrance to their hearts and help them to change inwardly. We who are priests know this well: our people may listen respectfully to our sermons and perhaps accept intellectually the truths we preach; but we shall produce no real inner change in our hearers unless they love us and see us as one who loves them.

Parents and teachers likewise know of the need for love. It is a basic principle of discipline that no punishment will make a change in a child's character unless the punisher is someone whom the child loves, someone whose love the child does not want to lose. Outward behavior can be controlled by fear alone, but the inner ideals and values which constitute character can be influenced only by love. This is a fact of human psychology, not merely a poetic fancy.

If then we are going to be true apostles to those around us—family, friends, neighbors and fellow-workers—they first must like us. If they are going to become a little better for having known us, they must find in us, however faint, a reflection of the charity of Christ. To know whether or not I do reflect that charity, there are a few significant questions I might ask myself.

Am I generous in making allowances for the failings of others? So often we excuse ourselves by saying, "I'm not perfect"; yet too often we expect others to be perfect. Everyone has his bad days. If someone is irritable or rude or inconsiderate, charity will remind me that he may be at low ebb physically, or he may be plagued by financial or domestic worries, or he may be suffering from a chronic unhappiness that makes him lash out like a wounded bear at those around him. Far from being aroused to anger by his conduct, I shall be moved rather to compassion for his hidden hurts, and shall respond with patient kindness rather than with reproof.

Am I free-handed in my bestowal of honest praise? In most people there is far more of good than of evil.

The things that most people do well are much more numerous than the things they do poorly. Evil stands out more prominently than good, and one failure can hide a dozen successes. But charity looks for the good and for the successes. Maybe the potatoes are burned, but charity will notice only how good the salad is, or how tasty the broccoli. There is no easier way in which we can contribute to the simple happiness of others than by a word of sincere commendation. Usually we are so quick with our criticism, so chary with our praise. Just begin to hand out a few honest compliments (there is no need for dishonest flattery) and see how people warm up to you.

Am I a good listener? There are so many persons burdened with problems and with worries who need the relief of someone to talk to, someone who will listen with a sympathetic ear and who will respect confidences. Probably we know from our own experience how hard it is to find a good listener. The moment we even hint at a problem, the other party begins to look at his watch and to fidget uncomfortably. If we can just listen sympathetically to others, without giving evidence of haste or boredom and with genuine interest in what they have to tell—charity is at work, we are making ourselves lovable.

Do I easily accept suggestions from others, and give them credit for their suggestions? Some individuals resent suggestions as though they were a reflection on their own intelligence; if they didn't think of it themselves, a suggestion can't be much good. Even if my own idea seems better, but no real harm will come from ditching it, it is an easy act of charity to say to the other person, "Yes, that's a good idea; let's do it that way."

Am I adaptable, able to change my plans easily for the convenience of others? If I am so compulsively attached to my own timetable that nothing, just nothing can be allowed to interfere—then charity many times will take a beating, and I probably am not as likeable a person as by nature I could be.

These are just a few of the questions I might ask myself, but perhaps these few will do for a beginning. If I can answer all of them honestly in the affirmative, then Christ walks with me, and finds me very helpful in His work.

XII

THE GOOD YOU DO

I

THAT IS a profitable question for us to ask ourselves as we prepare to go to bed at night: "What positive good did I do today?"

We said our daily prayers, yes. Perhaps also we prayed the rosary. It may be even that we began our day with Mass and Holy Communion. Quite likely we can look back and recall one or two sizeable temptations which we conquered—an unchaste thought dismissed, angry words suppressed before they escaped our lips, a choice bit of gossip kept to ourselves although we were dying to tell it.

All in all, we may feel that it was a pretty good day; not one of our best perhaps, but nothing to be ashamed of. And then out of the stillness of the night comes (let us hope) the voice of our Lord to jar our complacency: "Even so you also, when you have done everything that was commanded you, say, "We are unprofitable servants; we have done what it was our duty to do' " (Luke 17:10).

Much too easily do we forget that sanctity is a two-sided coin. Tails, we keep from sin and we give to God His due of love and adoration in prayer, in the Mass and in the sacraments. But, having thus exercised our soul and invigorated it with grace, we must turn the coin. Heads, we put into action the graces we have received, we make ourselves instruments in the hands of Christ for the doing of His work.

We do Christ's work any time when, for love of Him, we do something—be it ever so little—to ease our neighbor's burden. Usually it *will* be little things that we do. It is not every day that we have the opportunity to persuade a backsliding relative to go to confession, or a non-Catholic friend to join the instruction class, or a careless Catholic neighbor to send his children to catechism.

But we do have the opportunities, every day, for a multitude of small deeds of mercy that may swell to a surprising size as they are gathered into the heart of Christ. Do we realize for example that a smile and a "thank you" given to the sales person or the bus driver may be a source of grace and merit when given for the love of Jesus; especially if the sales person or the bus driver has treated us grumpily because of some private unhappiness of his own?

Then there is the lift that we can give to the spirit of another by a simple word of commendation, a word of praise. It may not be anything very notable that the other person has done, perhaps nothing more than new curtains on the kitchen window or a wax job on the car. Yet the mere fact of our having noticed, our one little drop of appreciation, can sweeten that other person's day.

And it is especially in such little acts of charity as these, that charity should begin at home. Many persons can be courteous and patient and affable and appreciative towards friends and towards strangers, without feeling any obligation to exhibit these same qualities towards the members of their own families. Most of us tend to take the people we love far too much for granted. A wife may be quick to criticize her husband's omissions and very slow to speak a word of thanks or of praise for his acts (even if rare) of helpfulness and thoughtfulness. A husband may unhesitatingly call attention to the lack of salt in the soup yet take no notice of the smoothness of the gravy or the tenderness of the pie crust.

Children too will bloom and extend themselves under the warmth engendered by words on commendation. Parents who take notice only of the defects in their children's undertakings, with never a word of praise for the partial successes or for the honest effort expended; such parents are robbing their children of happiness and laying the foundation for chronic feelings of inferiority.

In the family and out of the family, every day offers its own little opportunities for the practice of charity. Today it may be an offer to baby-sit for the young couple next door so that they may enjoy an evening out together. Tomorrow it may be a visit to a sick neighbor down the street or an acquaintance in the hospital—persons perhaps with no special claim upon us, who will therefore feel all the more pleased at our interest in them. Tomorrow it may be an offer to do the grocery shopping for the neighbor who cannot leave her children, or the offer of our car for picnic purposes to the family that has no car. Another time it may be an hour of our time spent in listening to someone else's troubles; an hour that we may consider wasted, but an hour which God will reckon otherwise.

There are chosen souls who have a highly specialized apostolate. The cloistered nun labors for Christ almost entirely through her prayers for souls. The bedridden patient's mission is one of suffering; he agonizes with Christ and by his pains gains grace and salvation for others.

Most of us however are called by Christ to the apostolate of active, interpersonal charity. Through us, through our little deeds of thoughtfulness, of helpfulness, of kindness, Jesus wills that His love should flow to others. To the degree that we make ourselves eager and questing instruments of His love, to that degree do we find life satisfying and rich.

Aside from prayer and abstention from sin, what good did I do today?

II

In almost any parish the women who are active workers will outnumber the men workers by five to one. It is only the parish bowling league that can count on a strong roster of male members. In civic affairs the story is much the same. If there is work that really needs doing, it is the women who can be counted upon. They are the ones who will volunteer, they are the ones who will follow through.

Men are great one-shot workers. They will labor hard to stage the annual parish festival or to serve the yearly mother-daughter breakfast. They will stand on cold street corners for the Old Newsboys' sale to raise money for Christmas baskets. But when there is a call for something that needs sustained interest and persevering work, the men are noticeable by their fewness.

Men are great joiners. The average man's wallet will carry at least half a dozen membership cards in as many different organizations. Yet seventy-five percent of the card bearers will do well to average one meeting a year. Men seem to be much better at joining than they are at doing.

The men of course have an answer. They have been out of the home all day at their work. In the evenings and on Saturday and Sunday they want a chance to enjoy their home a bit and to get caught up on odd jobs around the house. Women on the other hand are shut up all day in the home and are glad (say the men) to get out once in a while. Besides, a man's got to get his sleep at night; he can't take a nap in the afternoon like the wife can.

This argument would hold more water if there were not so many professional and business women who also work outside the home all day, yet find the time and energy for various forms of personal service to the Church and the community. Perhaps the evidence is too weak to support the conclusion, but it does seem that we men are just simply more selfish than our womenfolk.

If that is true, we are selfish to our own ultimate loss. There is in each of us the urge to creative action, the urge to achieve something worthwhile, the urge to "make our mark" upon the world. By selfishness (and its cousin, laziness) we can stultify that urge; we can live in a rut until we have forgotten what the beckoning horizon looks like. And when we live by a philosophy of "I've-got-my-own-troubles-let-others-take-care-of-theirs," life has lost much of its zest. Monotony besets us; we feel grumpy and discontented; we vegetate rather than live.

It even may be that we die younger. It is notorious that women have a longer life-span than men, by several years. There are several theories to explain this phenomenon, and perhaps it is rash to offer a new theory. But it does seem just barely possible that it is the wider interests of women and their greater generosity in the giving of themselves for the benefit of others, which add at least some of the extra years to their lives. "Boredom" never is listed as the cause of death on a medical certificate, but boredom (an offspring of sloth) can be a slow killer.

For parents of growing families their children are of course the primary apostolate. It would be misplaced charity to leave one's children with a baby sitter six nights a week in order to do community work. Yet *some* interest outside the home on the part of parents is a practical way to teach the children the meaning of the Mystical Body of Christ and to train them in a sense of social responsibility. Unfortunately however it isn't only the parents of growing families who so often shrug, "Am I my brother's keeper?" Too frequently the query of Cain is on the lips of single men and men whose families have been raised.

What can we do? We can approach our pastor and say, "Father, I'd like to do some really useful work for the parish. You name it." Given time to recover from his shock, the pastor should be able to offer a lead. Or we could stop in at the local office of our diocesan Catholic Charities and ask for some volunteer work to do. Hospitals need us, homeless children need us, the aged need us. It may be that our first job will be to organize a volunteer group of others like ourselves.

We could extend our services to the Confraternity of Christian Doctrine in the parish or in the diocese,

111

to teach religion to public school children or to organize a religious discussion club. We could join the Legion of Mary or the St. Vincent de Paul Society and practice the works of mercy. We could join the Christian Family Movement. Perhaps some organization to which we already belong is dying from lack of interest; we might go to the meetings and see what needs doing.

There is so much to be done if only we can pry ourselves loose from self. Whether or not it adds years to our physical life, it most certainly will invigorate our mind and soul.

XIII

RAISE UP YOUR HEART

I

FROM OBSERVATION it may be assumed that husband and wife do not speak much of their love for one another, once the honeymoon sparkle has settled to a quiet glow. This does not mean that their love has lessened. It means only that the more confident each partner is of being loved, the less need there is for words of reassurance. I have seen husbands and wives at public gatherings, separated in the crowd and yet now and then looking about to search each other out. Never far from each other's thoughts, a quick glance and a smile is their message of love. I know too of husbands and wives who spend quiet evenings at home together without exchanging any word of affection; comfortable and content simply to know that the other is there. Words have their place in the expression of love, but it is a minor place.

We can understand this wordlessness of love quite easily in our human relationships. Yet in our relationship with God we often overemphasize the importance of words. We know that prayer is defined as "the rais-

113

ing of the mind and heart to God," and we think of husband and wife exchanging glances across a crowded room. In spite of the definition, however, we still tend to put our reliance in words, lots of words. In the art of prayer words have their place. Speech as well as thought is a gift of God and is well used in His praise. Words are especially essential to group prayer, wherein we bear witness to our oneness in Christ. Nevertheless we can obscure the true meaning of prayer if, having recited lengthy sentences and paragraphs, we feel that we have discharged our full duty to God.

Instructing His disciples in the practice of prayer Jesus says, "But in praying, do not multiply words, as the Gentiles do; for they think that by saying a great deal, they will be heard; for your Father knows what you need before you ask him" (Matt. 6:7-8). As He goes on then to teach His disciples His own prayer, the Our Father, Jesus makes it plain that it is quality which counts, not quantity. Christ is not saying that long and wordy prayers are bad; He simply is emphasizing the fact that mind and heart rather than mouth are the basic organs of prayer. We may labor through several pages of printed prayers and, presuming a right intention, our efforts certainly will not be displeasing to God. Yet one single moment in which we have thought of God exclusively, thought of Him with love and gratitude, thought of Him with submissiveness to His will or with repentence for our sins;

one such moment may have been more pleasing to God than a prayer of many words.

If God is just below the surface of our thoughts (as any loved one is) moments such as these can and should punctuate our day quite frequently. Measured by the clock the total time encompassed by such quick casting of the heart's glance to God may be very small. But it is these moments which indicate a permanent *spirit* of prayer, an enduring love for God.

Besides mere wordiness, another defect that may creep into our prayer habits is that of self-centeredness. Our prayers may revolve around self rather than around God. The *Gloria* of the Mass gives us a clue here. We say to God, "We give Thee thanks because of Thy great glory." We thank God, not for what He has done for us, but just for being Who He is.

If nine-tenths of our prayers are prayers of petition, asking God for favors for ourselves, and only one-tenth are prayers of adoration, of love, of thanksgiving, of sorrow and reparation for sin—then our prayer time is sadly out of balance. Unquestionably God does want us to ask Him for what we need, thereby acknowledging our dependence upon Him. "Ask and it shall be given you," Jesus assures us even as He commands (Matt. 6:7). Especially does Jesus want us to ask Him for spiritual favors, for the graces we need to do His will and to get to heaven. He wills also that we practice charity by praying for the needs, particularly the spiritual needs, of others.

Nevertheless a prayer-attitude in which we and our wants would take precedence over God and His glory, would be to invert the true order of importance in prayer. In the perfect prayer, the Our Father, Jesus devotes the first half to praise of God: "Our Father, Who art in heaven, hallowed be Thy name. . . ." Most of the second half of the Our Father is given over to asking for forgiveness and grace: "Forgive us our trespasses. . . ." Just one short sentence in between is devoted to temporal requests: "Give us this day our daily bread." We could not do better than to follow that proportion in all our prayers. God's glory and our spiritual needs must outweigh our hunger for the goods of this life.

If our own pattern of prayer is built around this proportion; if the task of directing our mind and heart to God occupies us much more than attention to the niceties of words; above all if behind all our prayers there is this disposition: "What You want, God, is what I want too"—then truly we pray at our best.

II

Usually it is the persons who try hardest to pray well who find the most difficulty in prayer. Some persons pray but little. Others look upon prayer as a formal duty (like saluting the flag) to be discharged in set words at certain conventional times. Such persons are not likely to worry about distractions in prayer.

On the other hand there are those who see prayer in its true light, as a line of communication which we must keep open between ourselves and God. They see prayer as a channel through which our love flows to God and God's love back to us. They understand the meaning of the definition of prayer as "a lifting of the mind and heart to God," and realize that words are the least important element in prayer. By the very fact that they understand so well the true nature of prayer, such persons often are troubled by their own seeming inadequacies in prayer.

For most of us the big prayer-problem is that of distractions. Whether it be at Mass or during our rosary or our morning or night prayers, always it seems that we start out with good intentions, then suddenly find ourselves halfway through our prayers without any recollection of how we got so far. This is not surprising if we have come to prayer with a mind full of worry—some great anxiety oppressing us or some major decision facing us.

But the truth is that so often our distractions are concerned with such ridiculous trivialities; ridiculous at least compared with the majesty of the God in Whose presence we stand. "What shall I get for dinner today. . . . I wonder if that old dress is worth making over. . . . I must be sure to get the children to the dentist this afternoon. . . ." Or, "Let's see, how much will I have left from my pay check when I get the bills all paid this week? . . . If I change my grip on the club

117

just a little maybe I can correct that slice of mine. . . .
If Joe doesn't show up for bowling tomorrow night
it's going to be bad for our team. . . ." Silly thoughts,
aren't they, as maybe we kneel with downcast eyes for
our thanksgiving after Holy Communion?

The truth is that mental concentration is fatiguing,
and the mind seeks to relax, seeks to escape. Some people have greater powers of concentration than others,
but for the average person the attention span (the
length of time the mind can be pinned to one idea) is
comparatively short. This means that prayer is hard
work. It means that even the best of us will have trou-
ble disciplining our thoughts so that we can give undivided attention to God.

We know that God does not expect the impossible
of anyone. To pray well it is necessary only that we
have the intention to pray, that we eliminate avoidable
distractions (turn off the TV!), that we do direct our
mind and heart to God as well as we can, and bring
our mind back to God when we discover it wandering at a distance. It is only deliberate distractions that
vitiate prayer: conscious and unopposed excursions of
the mind to escape the "tedium" of the rosary or the
"boredom" of the Mass.

Not long ago a young mother called on me. I had
known her as a girl but had not seen her for some years.
She had gone out of her way to pay me this visit, and
I was both touched and pleased at this evident fondness

for her old pastor. Lacking a baby sitter, she had brought her three small children with her. They had the natural restlessness of children and our conversation was interrupted constantly by her efforts to keep the youngsters from pulling over a lamp or handling the bric-a-brac, by getting them a drink or taking them to the toilet. Actually her attention was on the children oftener than on me. Yet the very fact of her coming to see me in spite of such difficulties, gave evidence of the warmth of her feelings. When she left, shooing her three little distractions ahead of her, she left behind a bit of brightness for the rest of the day.

Similarly when we undertake to visit with God, we may spend a good part of our prayer time, perhaps most of it, in chasing after our restless, vagrant thoughts. The amount of actual attention that God gets may be small. Yet God is pleased with our efforts, pleased with our honest intention to talk with him. Indeed, the harder it is for us to pray, the more pleasing to God our prayer may be. Our very distractions are evidence to God of the warmth of our love for Him.

It is as though we said (and sometimes we can say nothing else), "Dear God, I do so want to talk to You of my love for You, of my trust in You and of my gratitude to You. I do so want to tell You of my needs and then quietly listen as You answer me with Your guidance and with Your strengthening love. But You can see that my mind just will not follow my will. I kneel in Your presence and all I can do is to keep chasing after my wandering thoughts. Please God, let my very distractions tell You that I love You." There is no dishonor to God in a prayer such as this.

XIV

GRACE IS WITH YOU

I

LITTLE JIMMY DREW A CUP of water from the faucet and poured the water on his dog's head. "I am baptizing you, Shep," Jimmy said; "Now you are a human being. Speak to me." Slowly Shep rose up on his hind legs until he was standing erect. "Well," Shep said, "I never have talked before. Just give me a little time to get used to it. I have a feeling that you and I are going to have a lot of fun together, Jimmy."

This incident never happened, of course, except in Jimmy's vivid imagination. However it is a good illustration of what did happen to you and to me when, in Baptism, God chose to share His own divine life with us. Before Baptism there was an impassable gulf between God and ourselves. We could not possibly enjoy what God enjoys, no more than a dog can enjoy a Christmas carol. We could not possibly communicate adequately with God nor God with us, no more than the master can share his innermost thoughts with his dog. For a dog to be able to think and speak and to share his master's loves and joys, the dog would have to be raised to the level of a human being. He would have to be given a human nature. For the dog this would be a *super* nature, a kind of existence above the nature of a dog.

Although Jimmy could not humanize his beloved Shep, God could and did divinize you and me. In Baptism God gave to us a *super* natural life, a kind of life above the nature of a human being. God raised us to His own level. He chose to share with us His own divine life.

The exact "how" of it must remain largely a mystery, until in heaven we discover fully what has happened to us. We do know that at Baptism God entered into our soul in a very special way. Joining our soul to Himself, He gives us the new kind of life which we call sanctifying grace. We do not cease to be human, we do not become little gods. But we do become God-like. With our new powers, what we say and do now reaches God and has value in His eyes. God in turn is able to reach us with His graces and inspirations, is able to guide and strengthen us. There is communication between God and ourselves.

Moreover we can begin to enjoy what God enjoys. Here and now we can share God's happiness only to a very limited degree. We can find joy in holiness and rich inner rewards in our love for neighbor and for God. Yet our soul is restricted in its divine activities by the necessity of working in and through a physical body. Even a humanized dog might find it difficult to play tennis or the violin with its animal's paws. For the full operation of this divine life in our soul, we must await the final act by which God's joy will become ours also. This will be when God confers upon us what theologians call "the light of glory." It is a special power which, added to the supernatural life that already is ours, will enable us in heaven to see God as He is. We shall be swept into a face-to-face, love-to-love union with God in heaven. It is then, in that moment of violent ecstasy, that the flea-scratching and bone-gnawing pleasures of earth will fade into insignificance.

In the meantime, assuming that we have the habitual desire to make our will one with God's, all that we say and do and think has an eternal significance. Because of our union with God, God Himself is working in us and with us in all that we do. Operating a punch press, vacuuming a rug, brushing our teeth—everything (sin excepted) is increasing in us the process of divinization, is enlarging our capacity for the final happiness that awaits us.

We can, of course, lose this divine life. We can refuse God the one small price that He asks in exchange for it: our love. That in effect is what we do if we reject God's will and, by grievous sin, choose self in preference to God. Yet even then the root of life is present in the form of the baptismal character. Just as the feebly pulsing heart of the rescued drowning victim cries out for a return of air to the lungs, so does

123

the baptismal character cry out for a return of the sinner to God. A humble and heartfelt "God I love You and because I love You I am sorry," is enough to bring life rushing back into the soul again.

This, much too briefly, is the story of sanctifying grace. It is a story which we need often to recall. If we let ourselves think of sanctifying grace as a vague theological abstraction, then we shall lose nine-tenths of the zest of Christian living. This divine life in us is more real than the blood in our veins. It should flavor our every waking moment. Without this divine life the greatest man in all the world is, in God's sight, of less account than the humblest laborer whose soul is in the state of grace. One man may build a skyscraper and his work count less than a dunghill. Another man may drive a single nail and the sound of his hammer be heard in heaven. Who of us, established in union with God, can feel that his or her life counts for little?

II

Unless we are far advanced in sanctity, we have more than a grain of spiritual conceit. We overcome a temptation and we feel quite proud of ourselves. We do an act of genuine charity and we fairly glow with self-approval. True, this is not wholly a matter of conceit. It is the function of a good conscience to commend us when we have done well, as it also is the role of conscience to reprove us when we have done evil.

Yet we are prone to magnify by several decibels the approving voice of conscience. The reason why we seldom give God full credit may be that we so often do not advert to the magnitude of God's concern for us, the persistence with which He pursues us with His grace.

Now and then we are able to see God's helping hand in some circumstance of our life; as when, faced by a strong temptation and on the verge of surrender, something saves us from collapse. Perhaps the temptation itself is taken away, or a circumstance intervenes to make the sin impossible or no longer desirable. As we stand almost trembling from the closeness of our call, we know that it is a power outside of us which has rescued us.

It is not always in matters of sin and temptation that we can detect God's grace at work. Sometimes we plan a course of action that seems attractive to us. It even may be a course of action that appears useful and necessary, such as the buying of a certain house or the getting of a certain job. Then obstacles arise that defeat our purpose. At the moment we are bitterly disappointed, but the day comes when we look back and see how fortunate it was that our plan did not succeed. As things turned out, we are ever so much better off. God's view is the long view, and His plan for us is a lifetime plan, not a five- or a ten-year plan.

All of us can find instances such as these in our lives.

What we may forget however is that for every time God's hand comes openly into view, there are a thousand other times when His hidden hand is just as actively at work. God *never* forgets us, never takes His mind off us, never leaves us alone.

The day-to-day and moment-to-moment helps which God gives us, we call actual graces. These actual graces may take a limitless number of forms. God may see to it that we read a certain book which will have a special meaning for us or that we hear a sermon whose message we particularly need. God may lead us to encounter a specific person who will influence us for good, or He may take away a friend whose companionship may ultimately be hurtful. Accordingly as it will contribute to or against our best interests, God may steer us toward or away from this or that job, or place or event. Nothing that touches us is unimportant to God.

The person of good will, established in sanctifying grace and trying prayerfully to make his decisions and solve his problems as best he can, is receiving actual graces all his waking moments. With a little push here and a gentle nudge there, God continually is guiding him towards heaven. Even the sinner lives and moves amid a ceaseless bombardment of grace. In the case of the sinner, God's anxious care has but one objective: to find a chink in the shell of self wherein His grace may find entrance and the sinner be aroused to repentance. Only when that step has been taken can other graces become operative and God's guidance fully effective.

In His lavish bestowal of actual grace, God still respects the free will with which He has endowed us. The interaction of grace and free will is one of those mysteries which we can hope to understand fully only when we look into the divine Mind in heaven. Here, with our limited created intellects, we can grasp but dimly God's ways of dealing with His creatures.

Searching for an example which will give us some concept of the relationship of grace and free will, we may take the modern automobile equipped with power steering. In such a car we have only to touch the wheel lightly, with a finger, in order to turn the car in the desired direction. Similarly, in our good deeds and our conquests of temptation, it is God's grace which does most of the work. Yet it remains for us to give that last little touch which puts grace to work or leaves grace unused.

It would be stupid ever to feel smug because, powered by grace, we have done something good. God is pleased and God will reward us, but He Himself has done most of the work. It would be equally foolish ever to succumb to discouragement. If I honestly can say, "I have done my best," then I have done all that God asks of me. In His own time and way, God will do the rest.

FIDES **DOME** BOOKS

D-1 GROWTH OR DECLINE, Emmanuel Cardinal Suhard. The State of the Church in the Modern World. (95¢)

D-2 MORE THAN MANY SPARROWS, Leo J. Trese. A Practical Guide to Christian Living. (95¢)

D-3 WHAT CATHOLIC GIRLS SHOULD KNOW ABOUT MARRIAGE, Francis X. Dietz. A Review of Catholic Teaching on Marriage. (95¢)

D-4 ACCENT ON PURITY, Joseph E. Haley, C.S.C. An Illustrated Guide to Sex Education. (95¢)

D-5 WISDOM SHALL ENTER, Leo J. Trese. A Course in Catholic Apologetics. (95¢) With Discussion Questions.

D-6 MENTAL HEALTH IN CHILDHOOD, Charles L. C. Burns. A Nontechnical Discussion of Problems with Maladjusted Children. (95¢)

D-7 PRIESTS AMONG MEN, Emmanuel Cardinal Suhard. On the Priestly Mission in the Modern Social Order. (95¢)

D-8 PURITY, MODESTY, MARRIAGE, Joseph Buckley, S.M. A Christian Design for Sex. (95¢)

D-9 SIGNS OF LIFE, Francis Louvel, O.P. and Louis J. Putz, C.S.C. The Seven Sacraments. (95¢) With Discussion Questions.

D-10 CHRISTIANS AROUND THE ALTAR, The Community of St. Severin. The Mass as the Sacrament of Unity. (95¢)

D-11 MODERN MORAL PROBLEMS, Msgr. J. D. Conway. Catholic Viewpoint on Controversial Questions. (95¢) With Discussion Questions.

D-12 MANY ARE ONE, Leo J. Trese. Christ in Daily Life. (95¢) With Discussion Questions.

D-13 WHAT IS YOUR VOCATION? Brother Andre, S.C. and Joseph H. Maguire. A Guide to the Priesthood, Religious Life, Marriage, and the Single Life. (95¢) With Discussion Questions.

D-14 THE TRIUMPH OF CHRIST, A. M. Henry, O.P. The Word Made Flesh. (95¢)

D-15 THE MEANING OF MARRIAGE, Eugene S. Geissler. Sex, Love, and Life—I. (95¢) With Discussion Questions.

D-16 THE MEANING OF PARENTHOOD, Eugene S. Geissler. Sex, Love, and Life—II. (95¢) With Discussion Questions.

D-17 WHAT THEY ASK ABOUT SIN, Msgr. J. D. Conway. Moral Theology, the Commandments, and the Virtues. (95¢)

D-18 THE ADOLESCENT BOY, W. Connell, S.J. & J. McGannon, S.J. Trying To Get His Point of View. (95¢)

D-19 CONVERSATION WITH CHRIST, Peter-Thomas Rohrbach, O.C.D. An Introduction to Mental Prayer. (95¢)

D-20 LEND ME YOUR HANDS, Bernard F. Meyer, M.M. A Popular Guide for Parish Catholic Action. ($1.25) With Discussion Questions.

D-21 THE CREED—SUMMARY OF THE FAITH, Leo J. Trese. Volume I of the Faith and Christian Living Religion Program. ($1.25) With Discussion Questions.

FIDES **DOME** BOOKS

D-22 SALVATION HISTORY AND THE COMMANDMENTS, Leo J. Trese and John J Castelot, S.S. Volume II of the Faith and Christian Living Religion Program. ($1.25) With Discussion Questions.

D-23 THE SACRAMENTS AND PRAYER, Leo J. Trese. Volume III of the Faith and Christian Living Religion Program. ($1.25) With Discussion Questions.

D-24 GUIDE TO CHRISTIAN LIVING, Leo J. Trese. Volume IV of the Faith and Christian Living Religion Program. ($1.25) With Discussion Questions.

D-25 THE PSALMS, Fides Translation. Introduction by Mary Perkins Ryan. A Clear, Modern Translation. ($1.25)

D-26 MARRIAGE IS HOLY, H. Caffarel. Essays on the Spiritual Aspects of Marriage. ($1.25) With Discussion Questions.

D-27 MORNING PRAISE AND EVENSONG, William Storey. A Popularization of the Two Major Hours of the Office. ($1.25)

D-28 A MAN APPROVED, Leo J. Trese. The Priest and His Vocation. (95¢)

D-29 ST. PAUL—APOSTLE OF NATIONS, Henri Daniel-Rops. A Fast-moving Biography of St. Paul. (95¢)

D-30 WOMAN IN THE MODERN WORLD, Eva Firkel. An Appeal to Feminine Human Nature. (95¢)

D-31 YOU ARE NOT YOUR OWN, Dennis J. Geaney, O.S.A. The Mystical Body in Action. (95¢)

D-32 THE MEANING OF GOD, Emmanuel Cardinal Suhard. The Meaning of God, God's Providence, The Christian Family and the Parish Community. (95¢)

D-33 FOR MEN OF ACTION, Yves De Montcheuil. Spiritual Guidance for the Layman. (95¢)

D-34 SEEDS OF THE DESERT, Rene Voillaume. Like Jesus at Nazareth. (95¢)

D-35 GOD SPEAKS TO MEN, Thomas Barrosse, C.S.C. Understanding the Bible. (95¢)

D-36 THE MODERN APOSTLE, Louis J. Putz, C.S.C. About the Vocation of the Layman in the Church. (95¢)

D-37 WHAT THEY ASK ABOUT THE CHURCH, Msgr. J. D. Conway. Intelligent Answers to Questions Asked About the Church. ($1.25)

D-38 YOU SHALL BE WITNESSES, Dennis J. Geaney, O.S.A. The "New Spirituality" of the Catholic Layman in the Modern World. (95¢)

D-39 BOOK FOR BOYS, Leo J. Trese. Practical and Concrete Advice on a Variety of Subjects for Young Boys. (95¢)

D-40 PROTESTANT HOPES AND THE CATHOLIC RESPONSIBILITY, George Tavard. A Primer on the Ecumenical Movement. (75¢) With Discussion Questions.

D-41 THE EUCHARISTIC PRAYER, J. A. Jungmann, S.J. An Analysis of the Canon of the Mass from the Pastoral Point of View. (75¢)

CPSIA information can be obtained
at www.ICGtesting.com
Printed in the USA
LVHW081127150322
713473LV00004B/153

9 781014 620200